BROWNIE GIRL SCOUT
HANDBOOK

Brownie Girl Scout Handbook
Girl Scouts of the USA
420 Fifth Avenue
New York, N.Y. 10018-2798

Let's Get Started!

Who is a Brownie Girl Scout? You are, and so are about one and a half million other girls in every part of this country and some other places, too.

Girl Scouting is different from every other kind of group that you can join. You won't find it like school, or like soccer practice, ballet lessons, art classes, the community center, or any of the other activities that you enjoy. As a Brownie Girl Scout you will have tons of chances to learn new things, make great new friends, and figure out what's important to you. You will also find out how to make your neighborhood, your country, and the world a better place to live, work, and play. Most of all, you'll have fun. Read on and see just what Brownie Girl Scouting is all about!

How Did Girl Scouting Get Started?

Girl Scouting was started in the United States in 1912 by a woman named Juliette Gordon Low. Her nickname was "Daisy," and she was a very special person. Here is her photo album:

Juliette Low

ALBUM

I was born in Savannah, Georgia, on October 31, 1860.

This is the house I grew up in. If you come to Savannah, you can visit my house.

Can you find Savannah, Georgia, on a map of the United States?

I had three sisters and two brothers. I was the second oldest.

I loved the arts.

I designed my own clothes, painted china, and performed skits with my family and friends.

I also liked roughhousing with my brothers. Once, just for fun, I allowed my cousin to braid a hunk of taffy into my long thick hair. But I wasn't laughing when my mother had to cut my braid off to get rid of the taffy.

I always loved animals. I kept coming home with stray dogs, cats, and even horses.

After I finished school, I married a man named William Low.

To celebrate our marriage, friends threw rice. A grain of rice got stuck in my ear. I had lost hearing in one ear as a child, and when the doctor tried to remove the rice, he damaged my good ear. From then on, I had very little hearing.

After our wedding, we lived in England and then Scotland. (Can you find England and Scotland on a map of the world?) Our marriage was an unhappy one. When I was 44, William died.

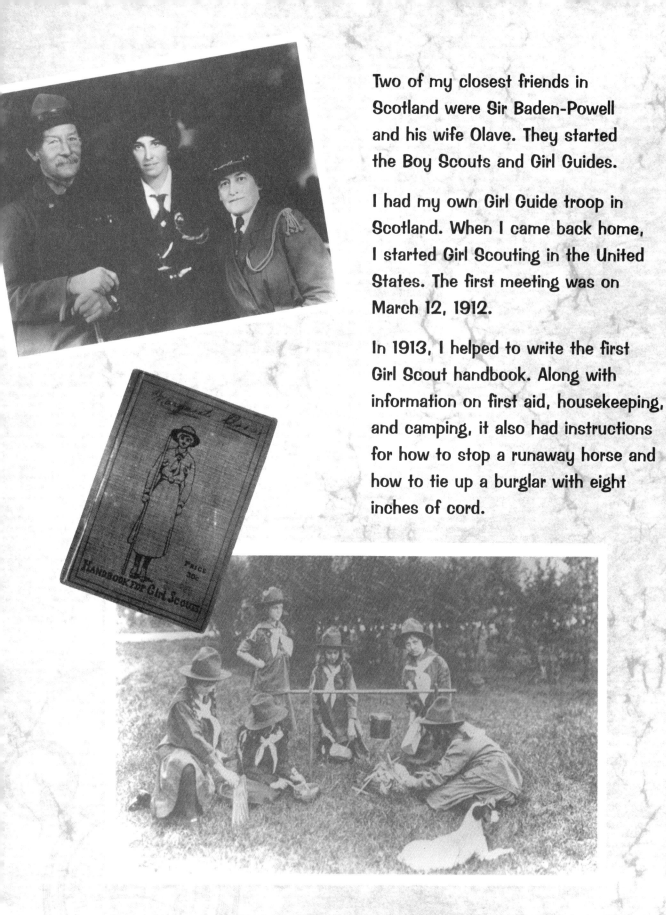

Two of my closest friends in Scotland were Sir Baden-Powell and his wife Olave. They started the Boy Scouts and Girl Guides.

I had my own Girl Guide troop in Scotland. When I came back home, I started Girl Scouting in the United States. The first meeting was on March 12, 1912.

In 1913, I helped to write the first Girl Scout handbook. Along with information on first aid, housekeeping, and camping, it also had instructions for how to stop a runaway horse and how to tie up a burglar with eight inches of cord.

The girls in my first U.S. troop learned to play basketball, went camping, and studied nature.

In 1927, Daisy died. She was 66 years old. At that time there were nearly 140,000 Girl Scouts in the United States. Today, there are more than two and a half million (2,500,000), and that number doesn't include all the grown-ups who help make Girl Scouting great!

ACTivity! Here's a crossword puzzle to try. All the answers can be found in Juliette's photo album. Otherwise, see page 42 for the ones you just can't get.

Across:

1. Her friends, the Baden-Powells, started the Boy Scouts and Girl _____.
6. Juliette's Girl Scout troop played _____.
7. Juliette was one of _____ kids.
8. The first Girl Scout meeting ever was held on _____ 12, 1912.

Down:

2. Juliette had her own Girl Guide troop in _____.
3. Because rice got in her ear, she had some _____ loss.
4. Juliette grew up in Savannah, _____.
5. Her nickname was _____.

What Does a Brownie Girl Scout Do?

No matter where they are, or what they do, all Girl Scouts have a few things in common. They all make the Girl Scout Promise. And they all try to live by the Girl Scout Law.

The Girl Scout Promise

On my honor, I will try:

To serve God and my country,

To help people at all times,

And to live by the Girl Scout Law.

What does the Girl Scout Promise mean?

On my honor, I will try—This means that you promise to do your very best.

To serve God—There are many ways to serve God. You might go to a religious service or live in peace with other people.

And my country—You can serve your country by saying the Pledge of Allegiance, reminding parents and other adults to vote on Election Day, or even sending a holiday card to military people overseas.

To help people at all times—You can carry a package for a neighbor, or help a friend with her homework. You might plant a tree or visit a nursing home with your troop.

The Girl Scout Law

I will do my best to be

   honest and fair,

   friendly and helpful,

   considerate and caring,

   courageous and strong, and

   responsible for what I say and do,
and to

   respect myself and others,

   respect authority,

   use resources wisely,

   make the world a better place, and

   be a sister to every Girl Scout.

ACTivity! There are 10 main parts to the Girl Scout Law. Go over each of them with a grown-up. Find or draw pictures that show people doing each of the 10 parts of the Girl Scout Law. Or list examples of how people can do each part. Paste, tape, draw, or write your examples in the chart below:

THE GIRL SCOUT LAW

I will do my best to be:

Honest and fair,	Friendly and helpful,
Considerate and caring,	Courageous and strong, and
Responsible for what I say and do	And to respect myself and others

Sharing songs is just one of the things Girl Scouts do. Here's a song for you to sing with your sister Girl Scouts.

Brownie Smile Song

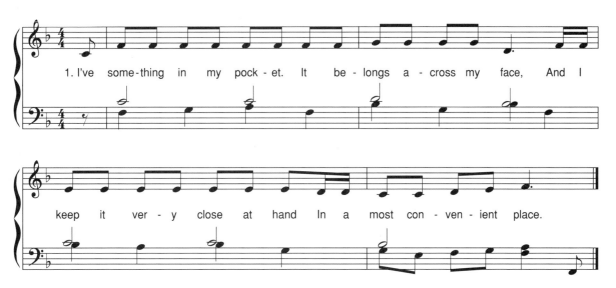

1. I've some-thing in my pock-et. It be-longs a-cross my face, And I keep it ver-y close at hand In a most con-ven-ient place.

2. I'm sure you couldn't guess it
   If you guessed a long, long while.
   So I'll take it out and put it on—
   It's a great big Brownie Smile!

Respect authority,	**Use resources wisely,**
Make the world a better place,	**And be a sister to every Girl Scout.**

What Makes Girl Scouting Special?

One way to show others how special it is to be a part of Girl Scouting is by wearing your Brownie Girl Scout uniform. Look at the different ways you can wear your Brownie Girl Scout uniform pieces.

In addition to the Girl Scout Promise and Law and the Brownie Girl Scout uniform, many other things make Girl Scouting special.

The Girl Scout sign is made when you say the Girl Scout Promise. Hold the three middle fingers of your right hand up as shown in the picture below.

The Girl Scout handshake is the way some Girl Scout friends greet each other. Shake hands with your left hand while making the Girl Scout sign with your right hand.

In a **friendship circle**, you stand in a circle with other girls. Place your right arm over your left arm. Hold hands with the girls next to you.

A **friendship squeeze** begins when you hold hands in a friendship circle. One girl starts. With her right hand she squeezes her neighbor's hand. Then that girl squeezes with her right hand. One by one, each girl passes on the squeeze until it travels all around the circle.

The **Girl Scout motto** is "Be Prepared." Girl Scouts try to be ready for any situation. And to be able to help those in need.

The **Girl Scout slogan** is "Do a good turn daily." Girl Scouts try to help others every day.

Special Days in Girl Scouting

Do you celebrate special holidays? Girl Scouts also have some special days.

October 31

Juliette Low's birthday (also known as "Founder's Day"). Juliette Low founded the Girl Scouts. To find out more about her, see pages 2-7.

Here are some ways to celebrate Juliette Low's birthday:

- Throw a party in her honor. Invite another troop. Do some activities that Juliette enjoyed—perhaps painting or putting on a skit. You can also make paper dolls, learn how to dribble a basketball, or be kind to animals.
- Put on a play that teaches other people about Juliette.
- Go to the Just for Girls Web site (www.girlscouts.org/girls) and find out more about Juliette.

February 22

Thinking Day is the birthday of both Robert Baden-Powell and his sister Agnes. They lived in England and started the first troop of Boy Scouts and Girl Guides. This is a special day for Girl Scouts and Girl Guides everywhere to think about each other.

Here are some ways to celebrate Thinking Day:

- Invite a Girl Scout who has traveled to or lived in another country to share her stories with your troop.
- Do a Thinking Day activity that you find on the Just for Girls Web site.
- Make a Thinking Day card that celebrates Girl Scouting and send it to a friend.
- Learn about the traditions of people in another country.

March 12

This is the Girl Scout birthday. On this date in 1912 in the United States, the first 18 girls officially registered as Girl Scouts.

  You may celebrate the Girl Scout birthday by:
• Learning to play basketball (a sport the first Girl Scouts played!).

• Visiting the Girl Scout Virtual Museum (www.girlscouts.org/organization/vmuseum/index.htm) and finding out what girls wore and did in 1912.
• Having a party! Invite friends who are not Girl Scouts. Share Girl Scout activities with them.

April 22

Girl Scout Leader's Day is the time to thank your leader for all the work she has done and for all the help she has given you.

  Here are some ways to celebrate Girl Scout Leader's Day:
• Make a card for your leader.
• Make a present for her.
• Make up a song for her.
• Write a poem to honor her.
• With other girls, plan a party for her.

Celebrating with a Ceremony

Girl Scouts hold ceremonies for many reasons: to celebrate a special day in Girl Scouting, to share feelings, or to highlight an accomplishment. Girl Scout ceremonies can be short or long. They can take place indoors or outdoors.

Your ceremonies can include Brownie Girl Scouts, other girls in Girl Scouting, Girl Scout leaders, other Girl Scout adults, and special guests like family and friends.

As the ceremony opens, everyone learns the reason for being there. You can begin a ceremony with:

- The Pledge of Allegiance.
- The Girl Scout Promise and Law.

The celebration takes place in the middle of the ceremony. Some ways to celebrate are to:

- Light candles. You can also use flashlights.
- Sing songs or do a special dance.
- Recite poems.
- Read special sayings or describe how different religions might express thanks.
- Tell or act out stories.

The closing is the time to thank guests and say goodbye.

After you have learned the Girl Scout Promise and Law, you are ready to be *invested*. This means you will participate in a ceremony in which you state the Girl Scout Promise, say the Girl Scout Law, and receive the Brownie Girl Scout pin. You might also sing songs or put on a skit to show how well you know the true meaning of Girl Scouting.

A Special Place

The Juliette Gordon Low Girl Scout National Center, also known as "The Birthplace," is the house in Savannah, Georgia, where Juliette Low was born. This house has been turned into a museum. People can visit it to learn about Juliette Low's life. Junior, Cadette, and Senior Girl Scout troops can take part in many fun activities there. As a Brownie Girl Scout, you can look forward to visiting the Birthplace when you are older.

Girl Scouting All Over the World

There are Girl Scouts in other countries, too. Some are American girls living overseas. Either their parents work for the U.S. military or for companies in foreign countries. You might be one of them. Girls in many foreign countries can also be Girl Scouts. They are often called Girl Guides. Girl Scouting is part of the World Association of Girl Guides and Girl Scouts (WAGGGS, for short).

Girl Scouts and Girl Guides all around the world also make their own Girl Scout Promise. They may say different words, but each one promises to be her best each day.

Girl Scouts and Girl Guides from other countries wear uniforms, too. Some look like yours. Others are very different.

World Centers

WAGGGS has four world centers— Our Cabaña in Mexico, Our Chalet in Switzerland, Pax Lodge in England, and Sangam in India. Perhaps you'll visit these world centers when you get older.

Mexico

Switzerland

England

India

Brownie Girl Scout Insignia

Girl Scout insignia are awards, patches, and emblems you wear on your uniform to show that you are a Girl Scout and the activities you have done.

The Brownie Girl Scout Pin tells others that you are a Brownie Girl Scout. It is shaped like a trefoil, or "three leaves." Each leaf stands for one part of the Girl Scout Promise. In the middle of the pin is a brownie elf. You may wear your Brownie Girl Scout Pin even when you are not wearing your uniform.

The World Trefoil Pin shows that you are part of the World Association of Girl Guides and Girl Scouts (also known as WAGGGS). You may wear it on your regular clothes as well as on your uniform. The golden trefoil on a blue background represents the sun shining over all the children of the world.

The Bridge to Brownie Girl Scouts Award is for girls who were once Daisy Girl Scouts and did special activities before becoming Brownie Girl Scouts. The rainbow represents going from one Girl Scout level to the next.

The **Girl Scouts USA strip** shows that you are part of the family of Girl Scouts in the United States of America.

The **Girl Scout council strip** shows the name of your Girl Scout council. People in a council make Girl Scouting possible for you. Every Girl Scout troop has its own number. The number is given to your troop by your Girl Scout council.

The **membership star** stands for each year you are a Girl Scout. The color of the circle behind the star tells the age level. The color green shows that you got the star as a Brownie Girl Scout, and a blue disc shows that you were once a Daisy Girl Scout.

Brownie Girl Scout Awards

You receive the following awards for doing special Girl Scout activities:

Brownie Girl Scout Try-Its are earned for doing activities on a specific topic. Try-Its are one of the fun parts of being a Brownie Girl Scout. You can find them in *Try-Its for Brownie Girl Scouts*. Lots of times you'll do Try-Its with your whole troop, which doubles the fun. This handbook and *Try-Its for Brownie Girl Scouts* are linked chapter by chapter. If you enjoy reading a particular chapter in this book, go to the same chapter in the Try-Its book.

Try activities based on things you like to do or on new things you'd like to learn.

Religious awards are given by many religious groups for girls of their faith who are Girl Scouts. You can find out about these awards from your Girl Scout leader or your religious group.

The Brownie Story

This story was adapted from a tale told at the beginning of Brownie Girl Scouting in 1926.

Mary and Tommy lived with their father and grandmother in a cabin near the woods. Their father worked very hard all day. Their grandmother was too old to do the housework. Their father tried his best to keep the house clean. Mary and Tommy didn't help him very much. They just played all day long.

"What this house needs is a brownie or two," said their grandmother, looking around the messy house.

"What is a brownie, Granny?" asked Mary.

"A very helpful little person," answered their grandmother. "She'd come in before the family was up and did all sorts of chores. The brownie always ran off before anyone could see her, but they could hear her laughing and playing about the house sometimes. Brownies always helped for love."

"Oh, Granny, where are the Brownies now?" asked Tommy.

"Only the Wise Old Owl knows, my dear."

That night, Mary could hardly sleep. She kept thinking about the brownie. "There's an owl living in the old shed by the pond," she thought. "If it is the Wise Old Owl, she can tell me where to find a brownie." Mary got out of bed and hurried to the pond in the woods.

"Hoo! Hoo!" said a voice behind her.

"It's an owl! Maybe it's the one I'm looking for," said Mary. "Please," asked Mary of the owl, "where can I find a brownie to come and live with us?"

"Well, Mary," said the owl, "I can tell you how to find one of the brownies. Go to the pond when the moon is shining and turn yourself around three times while you say this charm:

'Twist me and turn me and show me the elf.

I looked in the water and saw _____.'

Then look into the pond to see the brownie. When you see the brownie, you will think of a word that ends the magic rhyme."

Mary turned and ran to the pond. She slowly turned herself around three times while she said the rhyme:

"Twist me and turn me and show me the elf.

I looked in the water and saw _____."

She stopped, looked into the pond, and saw only her own face. "Belf! Helf! Jelf! Melf!" All those words rhymed with elf but they didn't mean anything. Suddenly, she gasped. "Myself! I see nothing but myself. I'm a Brownie!" said Mary.

Mary went home and back to bed. In the early morning, she told Tommy what had happened. Together they crept downstairs and did every bit of work they could find to do before their father woke up. Then they hid in the kitchen so he wouldn't see them.

When Father came downstairs, he looked around and rubbed his eyes. The table was set, the floor was clean, and the room was as bright and shiny as a new penny.

At first, Father could not say a word. Then he ran to the foot of the stairs, shouting, "Mother! Our brownie has come back!"

"Thank Goodness!" said Grandmother. "Where is she?" Father heard laughter coming from the kitchen.

"It must be the brownie," he said. He opened the kitchen door, and saw Mary and Tommy dancing around the room.

"What's this?" he asked, his eyes twinkling. "Where are the real brownies?"

"Here we are!" yelled Mary and Tommy as they ran into their father's arms.

Now here's a modern "Brownie" story.

A Brownie Tale

Sara was sad. She couldn't go with her sister on the overnight trip. Her father was changing a tire on the family car and wouldn't let her help him. He said she wasn't big enough. "I can't do anything," Sara said to herself. So she sat on the park bench and felt sorry for herself.

A brownie overheard her. "She is not happy," the brownie thought to herself. "She wants to be more helpful, but she doesn't know what to do." Since brownies like to show children how to be helpful, this brownie decided to visit Sara.

"Look at this park. Isn't it a mess? " the brownie said. She was staring over Sara's shoulder.

Sara turned around quickly. "Who are you?" She asked.

"I am a brownie."

"What's a brownie?"

"A brownie is a girl who wants to be helpful to others."

"How can I be helpful?" Sara asked. "I'm too young to do almost everything."

"You're not too young. There are lots of things you can do."

"Like what?"

"As I was saying, look at this park. Isn't it a mess?" Sara looked around at the old newspapers and candy wrappers that littered the park.

"Yes, but what can I do about it?" Sara wanted to know.

"You can get your friends to help you clean up the park," the brownie said.

"I guess I can," Sara said.

The next day at school, she got her teacher and some friends to pull on some gardening gloves and help her collect litter from the park.

A few days later, Kim was walking home from school. She was feeling sorry for herself, too. She kicked a stone from the sidewalk and watched it land on the lawn of a nearby nursing home. "There's nothing to do," she said. "I'm bored."

"I can help you with that," the Brownie said to her.

"Who are you and where did you come from?" Kim asked.

"I am a brownie. A brownie is always around to show people how they can be helpful."

"What are you talking about?"

"You said you were bored. Have you ever thought about helping other people?"

"Why should I?" Kim replied.

"Because when you help others, you help yourself. Look at the nursing home you just walked by. There are lots of things you can do to help the people there."

"Like what?"

"Like visit them. Bake cookies with them. Plan a sing-along with them. Many things like that."

"That doesn't sound like a lot of fun to me. It sounds like a big waste of time."

"More of a waste of time than walking around bored?" the brownie asked.

"Oh, OK," Kim said. She went home and asked her family to help her plan a visit to the people in the nursing home. Sara and Kim had fun helping other people. They were sad when they had finished.

The following week Sara went to the park after school. She looked behind the park benches, in the bushes, and along the fence. Finally, the brownie appeared, near a small pond.

"I've been looking all over for you," Sara said.

"I was busy helping other people. There are so many things to do."

The brownie brushed the dirt off her brown tights. "I just finished helping someone plant a garden," she said.

"I want to do more to help others. What can I do?" Sara asked.

"Be here at noon on Saturday." With that the Brownie simply vanished.

Meanwhile, Kim looked for the brownie at the nursing home. She checked the front of the building, the parking lot, and in the garden. No brownie. Finally, Kim looked behind a large oak tree next to the building. There, like magic, the brownie appeared.

"How did you get here so fast?" Kim asked.

"Oh, I have a way of showing up when I am needed," the brownie answered. She straightened the lopsided brownie cap on her head.

"Brownie, my family and I did a sing-along at the nursing home. It was fun. Now I want to do something else. I like being helpful," Kim said.

"Meet me in the park at noon on Saturday."

The brownie disappeared with just sparkling dust left behind.

Saturday finally came. Sara and Kim waited for the brownie on separate park benches. Each wondered what the other was doing there. Soon, the brownie appeared.

She had traveled so fast that her cap had fallen off.

"You two are a lot alike," the Brownie said. "You have learned the value of helping other people. Now you can work together."

"We can?" Sara and Kim looked at each other shyly.

"Come with me," the Brownie said. The two girls followed her to a little pond.

"Turn yourself around three times while you say this charm:

'Twist me and turn me and show me the elf. I looked in the water and saw ___.'
When you see the brownie, you will think of a word that ends the magic rhyme," the
brownie said.

Both girls went to the pond and slowly turned themselves around three times
while they said, "Twist me and turn me and show me the elf. I looked in the water
and saw ___." When they looked in the water, each girl saw her own face. "Belf!
Helf! Jelf! Melf!" The girls tried all the words they could think of to rhyme with "elf."
Finally, they said it together. "Myself! I see myself! I saw myself! I'm a brownie now!"

Sara and Kim took each other's hands and danced around in a circle.

"Now you are both brownies. You can help each other think of ways to help other
people," the brownie said. With that, she disappeared in a puff of brownie dust.

Your Brownie Girl Scout Troop or Group

Your Brownie Girl Scout troop is a team that plans, plays, laughs, and learns together. But it is important for everyone to feel comfortable sharing ideas and practicing new skills. Girl Scouts have created some special ways to work together.

Lots of troops use a Brownie Girl Scout Ring. This allows the whole troop to share thoughts, ideas, and suggestions.

Remember to:

1. Share your ideas. Let people know what you think. If you feel shy, practice what you want to say in your mind before you say it.

2. Listen. Another girl's suggestion may help you think of a new idea.

3. Decide what you want to do as a group. Each girl should have an opportunity to speak. Everyone should have a say in the final decision.

4. Keep in mind that mistakes will happen and that having fun is very important.

Sometimes you might find that everyone is so excited about an idea that they are all talking at once. One solution to this problem is to use an object, like a stick, to indicate whose turn it is to speak. When one girl finishes, she can pass the object to the next girl. Or you might use the quiet sign. This means that someone raises her hand and stops talking. As others see her right hand in the air, they raise their hands too and stop talking.

One other tool to use in your troop is a *kaper chart*. This chart shows jobs that need to be done and who will do them. Each girl can volunteer. If everyone pitches in, this makes the work easier.

Every girl can be the leader of a group. But leaders have special responsibilities. They have to make sure that each person has a part in the activities. Sometimes that means letting someone else do something you wanted to do.

Troop Money

Your Brownie Girl Scout troop gets money for activities in different ways. There are troop dues and also money-earning projects like selling Girl Scout Cookies.

Girl Scout Cookie Sale Activity

Your troop may decide to sell Girl Scout Cookies as a troop project. This is a wonderful opportunity for you to learn some important skills that you'll be able to use for the rest of your life! If you would like to continue improving these skills, try earning the Girl Scout Cookie Sale Activity Pin. You can find the requirements in a booklet called the *Girl Scout Cookie Sale Activity Guide.* You will gain experience in:

- Introducing yourself to new people.
- Telling people about a project.
- Using math to add and subtract.
- Paying attention to safety rules.
- Answering questions.
- Learning how to set goals.
- Making decisions.

Look at the "Cookies Count" Try-It to get some ideas about selling cookies.

Remember!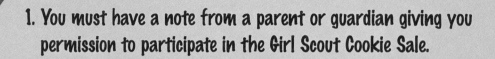

✔ 1. You must have a note from a parent or guardian giving you permission to participate in the Girl Scout Cookie Sale.

✔ 2. Your parent or guardian must always know where you are when you are helping with the cookie sale.

✔ 3. You must always have an adult with you when you sell cookies.

✔ 4. For safety reasons, you may not sell Girl Scout Cookies on the Internet. However, you may e-mail your friends and family to let them know about the sale.

Fun on the Job

There are lots of jobs connected with selling cookies and other products. Find out about some of them by taking a trip around the neighborhood with your leader or another adult. Go to a supermarket to find out how products are displayed. Visit a store and ask a salesperson to explain her job. Also ask her to suggest an idea to help you when you are selling Girl Scout Cookies.

Money Matters

After your troop has successfully earned some money, you'll all need to gather in your Brownie Girl Scout Ring to make some decisions!

ACTivity!   OUR PLAN

What do we want to do? ....
....

Where do we want to go? ....
....

How much will it cost? ....
....

When will we go or do this? ....
....

Who should join us? ....
....

Add It Up

Sometimes what you really want to do costs more than you have earned during the cookie sale. Here are some ideas for projects that will help you earn money:

• Making and selling printed note cards, stationery, and wrapping paper.

• Selling home-grown plants in decorated pots.

• Holding a tag or yard sale. (Each girl can contribute toys, books, dolls, and games.)

• Setting up a lemonade stand.

Can you think of some more?

Books You Might Like to Read

BOOKS

Bassachs, Anna Galera.
Celebrations: Creative Activities for Young Children. Monroe, Wash.:
Barrons Juveniles, 1998.

Livingston, Myra C.
Celebrations. New York:
Holiday House, 1985.

Rockwell, Anne F. *The Acorn Tree and Other Folktales.* New York:
Greenwillow, 1995.

Sierra, Judy. *Nursery Tales Around the World.*
Boston: Clarion Books, 1996.

Answers to crossword puzzle on page 7.

Chapter

2

TAKING CARE OF YOURSELF

Taking Care of Yourself

You are special—different from every other person in the world. No one has a body just like yours. Some girls are tall. Some girls are short. Some girls are thinner than others. As you get older, your body will change in many ways. There is no one best body. If you take care of the body you have, you'll feel good about yourself. And that's a feeling worth having!

Along with your body you have your very own mind. You make tons of decisions each day, like what cereal to have for breakfast or what shirt you want to wear with your favorite purple pants. Your body and mind must work together to keep you healthy. Eating right, exercising, enjoying hobbies, and making your own decisions are some of the ways that you can keep the one and only you in great shape.

Your Body Is One of a Kind

ACTivity! These activities will prove that no two people are exactly alike:

1. Tape pieces of newsprint (big sheets of paper) together to form a large sheet. Lie down on your back on it. Ask a buddy to take a crayon or marker and trace the shape of your body onto the paper. Draw in your face and clothing to complete this picture of you.

2. Find out what your fingerprints look like. On a piece of paper, with a soft, dark pencil, make a spot about the size of a quarter. Press one finger at a time on the spot and then press your fingers in the outline here. You can put clear tape over your fingerprints to keep them from getting smudged.

Compare your fingerprints with the fingerprints of other people. You should discover that no one has the same fingerprints as you do. Even if you could compare your fingerprints with those of people all around the world, you would never find an identical set.

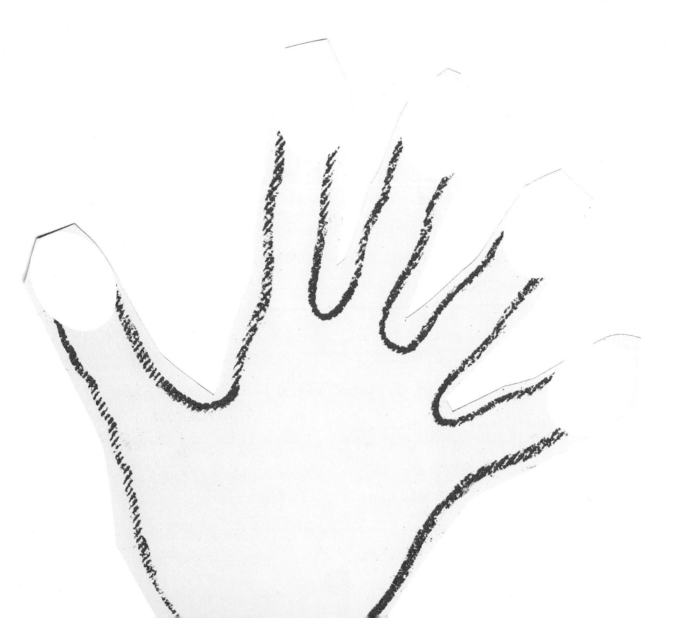

What's Next?

What can you do to keep your body and mind healthy and fit? The list below gives you some ideas. What can you add to it?

1. Exercise.
2. Eat healthy foods and drink lots of water.
3. Keep your body and clothing clean.
4. Sleep at least eight hours a night.
5. See your doctor and your dentist for regular checkups.
6. Make your own decisions.
7. Do the right thing.

Moving Parts

Run, jump, stretch, catch, throw, kick, and even laugh to exercise the muscles of your body. When you exercise you feel good—full of energy. You need to exercise. If you use all your free time to watch TV or chat on the phone, you may tire easily. That's not a very good feeling.

As you play sports or exercise more and more, your heart, lungs, and muscles will grow stronger. You'll be able to play sports better and longer.

Now is a great time to learn skills for sports. Playing sports is a fun way to spend your free time now and when you are older. Some girls participate in team sports like soccer, basketball, volleyball, or softball. Others prefer sports you can play without a team, like swimming, tennis, golf, in-line skating, and bicycling. Whatever sport you choose to play, it is important to practice the skills involved. For example, if basketball is your favorite sport, practice dribbling.

Sports Safety Tips

To play your sport better and longer, use the following safety tips:

1 Before you start your sport, loosen up your muscles with a few warm-up stretches.

Do upper body warm-up and stretching exercises.

• Start with shoulder rolls. Bring your shoulders up, back, and down. Repeat this four times. Stretch your arms over your head. Pretend that you are climbing a rope.

Do lower body warm-up and stretching exercises.

• Warm up and stretch the legs. March in place 16 times. Lift your knees up high 16 times. Kick up your heels 16 times. Now swing one leg and then the other out to the side like a hand on a clock 16 times.

2 Dress Right.

Wear the right shoes for your sport.

• Wear shoes with rubber cleats for soccer and softball. Wear court shoes for tennis.
• Wearing the right shoes will help keep you from slipping or turning an ankle.
• Make sure to tie the laces of your sneakers tightly.

Wear gear that will protect you from injury.

• Wear the right protective gear for the sport you are playing—for example, shin guards for soccer and a batting helmet for softball. A helmet must always be worn when riding on a bike or in-line skating.

Use equipment that is in good condition.

• Broken or worn-out equipment should not be used. Never try to adapt equipment that is not made for your sport.

3 Have a Partner.

Always exercise with another person.

• Whether you are riding your bike down the block or doing jumping jacks, have a friend along just in case one of you gets hurt.

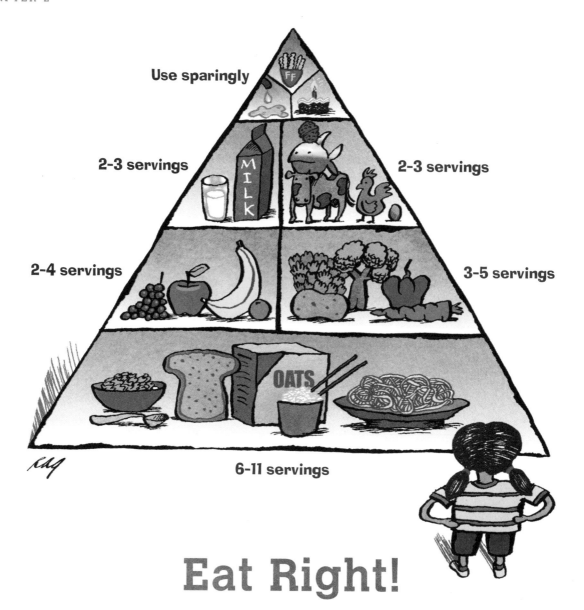

Use sparingly

2-3 servings

2-3 servings

2-4 servings

3-5 servings

6-11 servings

Eat Right!

Your body needs lots of different kinds of foods to stay healthy. The amount of each kind of food that you eat is also very important.

When you are being good to your body, you are giving it nutrients—what it needs to grow healthy and strong. Fresh fruits, vegetables, whole wheat and grains, beans, and milk have lots of nutrients. But potato chips, candy, sodas, and cake don't. Foods and drinks that contain lots of sugar, salt, and fats can cause you to gain too much weight and develop some serious health problems. You need fruits and vegetables, meat or other protein, milk or yogurt or cheese, breads, cereals, rice, and pasta, lots of water—juice is good, too—and just a little fat in your diet.

The food pyramid describes the types and amounts of food that you should eat to stay healthy.

ACTivity! Are you eating healthy foods? Are you eating the right amounts? In the space below, list everything you eat for breakfast, lunch, dinner, and snacks for one day. When you are done, compare what you ate with the suggested types of food and number of servings on the food pyramid.

How did you do? What do you need to change to eat in a healthier way?

What I Ate Today

Breakfast

Dinner

Lunch

Snack

ACTivity! Try the "Food Pyramid Party Mix" as a snack.
You will need:

- $1/2$ cup dried banana or apple chips.
- $1/4$ cup sunflower seeds.
- $1/2$ cup raisins.
- $1/2$ cup popcorn.
- $2/3$ cup granola.

Mix the ingredients in a serving bowl. This recipe serves about three people.

Be a Germ Fighter

Hygiene (pronounced just like "Hi Jean") means actions you take to stay clean. Use these tips and you are sure to be a champion germ fighter!

- Wash your hands often. It is especially important to wash them after you go to the bathroom, play with an animal, ride on public transportation, or play a sport.

- Use your own spoon, fork, straw, or glass. Germs on food can be passed from one person to another.
- Keep your clothes clean and dry. Don't stick wet clothes in the back of your closet or at the bottom of the hamper. Mold, a kind of fungus, can grow on wet clothing.

The Great Coverup

Clothes keep you warm, dry, and safe. But they also can be a way for you to express your very own sense of style.

Make them Wild, Make Them Serious, Make Them the Way You Want

ACTivity! Trace the figures and the clothes on pages 47-48. Decorate each piece. Dress these paper dolls for a party, a family reunion, or a day on the ball field. Use crayons, markers, glitter, glue, buttons, felt, scraps of material, and anything else. Cut out your tracings, making sure to keep the tabs on the clothes so that you can actually dress the figures. Make as many sets of paper dolls as you would like.

School Clothes

What are some of your favorite outfits to wear to school? (If you wear a uniform to school, think of your favorite outfits for the weekend.) What tops and bottoms look good together? Can you mix and match to make more outfits? Try them on.

Save time in the morning by choosing the clothes you will wear to school the night before. Fold them neatly or put them over a hanger so you can get dressed quickly in the morning.

Taking Care of Your Clothes

Ask an adult to help you learn:

- How to hand-wash clothing in a sink or basin.
- How to operate a washing machine.
- How to sort clothing to be washed. Learn what water temperature to use. Also learn which colors can be washed together and which colors need to be washed separately.
- How to organize clothes in closets and drawers.

Changes in Your Body

As you grow older, you will notice that your body changes. Parts of your body grow at different rates. You might notice that your nose or your feet look bigger. You may suddenly see changes in your body that make you look more grown up. Remember, everybody is different! And change is a normal part of being a human being!

ACTivity! Try making a time line that shows how you have grown over the years. Here are some suggestions for your time line. What other things can you include?
- My first birthday party
- My first day at school
- My first soccer game, dance recital, concert, or other special event

My Time Line ━━━

1 ....
....
....
....

2 ....
....
....
....

3 ....
....
....
....

TAKING CARE OF YOURSELF

4
....
....
....
....
....

5
....
....
....
....

6
....
....
....
....

7
....
....
....
....

8
....
....
....

9
....
....
....

55

Decision-Making

Make your own decisions. Sometimes your friends might want you to do something that makes you feel uncomfortable. Maybe they want you to hide from your younger sister when she wants to play with you. Or maybe they suggest that you sneak out to play after dark even though it is against your family's rules. Tell yourself that you, not your friends, know the best decision to make.

Practice making your own decisions by acting out the scenes on the next page. The more you practice, the easier it gets.

• Your teacher is sick and you have a substitute for the day. All the kids are acting silly and misbehaving. You try to do your work, but everybody is teasing you. What do you say?

• Your friend wants to borrow your favorite T-shirt, the one your mom and dad gave you for your birthday. It's special and something you take extra care with. How can you tell her no?

• The girl next door plays on a soccer team and you would really like to join. But your friends don't like her. What do you do?

Follow the Leader (That's You!)

Making your own decisions is one of the first steps toward becoming a leader. Other steps in the path to leadership are:

What Are Your Interests?

Making your own decisions also means choosing hobbies that are fun for you. If your best friend loves soccer, this does not mean you have to join a team, too.

Do you collect stuffed animals or basketball cards? Do you like to make things out of clay? Do you enjoy jumping rope? These are examples of hobbies. What are your hobbies?

As a Girl Scout you have lots of chances to work on hobbies. You might do Try-Its on different topics. Your troop might plan special activities or trips to learn new skills. And some people actually decide what they will be when they grow up based on a hobby they enjoyed as a child.

ACTivity! Try to match the hobbies in the column on the right with the careers in the column on the left:

Careers

Newspaper Reporter

Coach

Veterinarian

Park Ranger

Book Illustrator

Web Site Designer

Hobbies

Softball, Soccer, Tennis

Hiking

Drawing, Painting, Making Collages

Computer Games

Writing

Horseback Riding

Using Computers

Do you use a computer? When you say the word *computer*, you might be thinking about the one in the school library, at your parent's workplace, or maybe in your own home. But don't stop there! What about the calculator you use, the microwave oven in your kitchen, or the VCR with your TV?

Each of these products has a computer chip with instructions to do something with 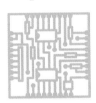 stored information. When you program your VCR to record, or your microwave to bake, you are using a computer chip. Can you find other computer chips at work in your home or community?

Software is a special program that tells the computer what to do.

You might use a word-processing program to:
- Record minutes of your troop meeting.
- Create a troop newsletter.
- Send a flier to parents.
- Make thank-you cards for people who buy Girl Scout Cookies.

You might use another kind of software to create documents called spreadsheets, which can:

- Keep track of troop funds.
- Keep track of dues.
- Make a list of expenses for a trip.

Or you might use other kinds of programs to:
- Play games.
- Look up things.
- Draw pictures.

Girls Online

There is a special place on the Internet just for Girl Scouts called Just for Girls. The address is www.girlscouts.org/girls. You can find a Brownie Girl Scout Try-It about using computers and a list of special Brownie Girl Scout "links" that will take you to selected sites on the Internet. There are also answers to questions, pictures of Juliette Low, and poems and artwork written by kids. You can even ask questions about something that's bothering you and get advice on a problem. Whenever you use the Internet, follow the safety rules shown on the Just for Girls Web site.

Me and the Media

What's your favorite TV show? Magazine? Commercial? Are there some that bother you? Listen closely to the things that are said and really look at the images to see if you agree or disagree with what is being shown.

You might turn off the TV if a show is making girls look silly or dumb. As long as you think about what's in the media (TV, books, magazines, radio, the Internet, and movies), you will always be one step ahead. If you want to learn more about how media work, read *Media Know-How for Brownie Girl Scouts.*

How Do You Feel About That?

You do not feel the same way all the time. Sometimes you feel happy. Sometimes you feel sad. You can also feel angry, scared, bored, excited, or surprised.

"Wow, that looks like something my four year old sister would draw," Tara said as she strolled by Amy's desk on Tuesday. Tears welled up in Amy's eyes but she didn't say anything to Tara. Instead she kept working on her picture. After everyone else left the room, Amy scribbled with black marker all over Tara's painting. She knew Tara would be very upset because the teacher had promised to put that particular painting in the show for parent's night next week. Amy didn't care. She was mad and she wanted to get back at Tara.

In this story, Amy's feelings were hurt. Rather than talking to her classmate, she chose to damage her artwork. Talking about your feelings, both good and bad, is extremely important. A parent, a Girl Scout leader, a teacher, a religious instructor, a brother or sister, or a friend are some people you can turn to when you feel bad. People who care about you want you to be happy. They can often help you to sort out your feelings and find ways to deal with different situations.

Focus on Feelings

ACTivity! Make a record of your feelings for a couple of days. Write about things that surprise you, scare you, anger you, or make you laugh or cry. Then choose one or two feelings and use them in a story. Create a setting and a plot. Have the main character experience the same feeling that you did. (But you can change the situation.)

Here are some ideas:
- Write about how you feel.
- Draw a picture.
- Listen to music.
- Dance or exercise.
- Read a book.
- Play a game.

Maybe the best advice is:
DO SOMETHING!

How do you feel?

Staying Safe

Learn what to do in emergencies and how to handle uncomfortable situations.

Safety Do's and Don'ts

Here are some Do's and Don'ts:

If someone makes you feel uncomfortable, or if you think someone will hurt you:

- DO RUN FOR HELP. Drop everything and run quickly.
- DO SHOUT FOR HELP.

When walking:

- DO walk with a friend
- DON'T take shortcuts through dark alleys, deserted buildings, or parks.

At home:

- DON'T answer a stranger's questions on the phone, even if the voice sounds friendly.
- DON'T tell anyone that you are home alone.
- DON'T open a door to a stranger.

When you are in the house by yourself, you should know some special rules to follow when you answer the phone.

- DO call a parent, a close neighbor you trust, or the police if you receive a phone call that worries you. Tell that person about the phone calls. Ask for someone to stay with you until the adults are home.
- DO call 911 or the emergency number in your community if you feel frightened.
- DON'T tell the caller that you are in the house by yourself. If he or she asks for your mom or dad, just tell the caller that your mom or dad cannot come to the phone right now.
- DON'T give out any information. Just ask for the name and phone number and say that someone will return the call. Some homes have Caller ID service and you can see the phone number of the person calling you. Tell the person you have the number and have written it down. Ask for the name and say that someone will call back later.

In parks and play areas:
- DO play where you can be seen by the person taking care of you.
- DON'T play in deserted, out-of-the way places, such as abandoned buildings, empty laundry rooms, storerooms, or rooftops.
- DON'T leave school grounds during breaks or recess.
- DON'T play around construction sites, mining sites, train yards, or any place with trucks.
- DON'T play in discarded refrigerators, sinks, or empty crates and boxes on the street or in an empty lot.

If a stranger approaches you:
- DON'T go near his or her car, even if the person says your mom or dad said it's OK.
- DON'T even get in a conversation.
- DON'T believe any message he or she gives you.
- DON'T take any candy, gum, or gifts.
- DON'T go with that person into an elevator or building.

When using public restrooms:
- DO take someone you know with you.
- DO lock the door to the restroom stall.
- DON'T talk to strangers or let them near you.

If you see something suspicious or a stranger approaches you, try to remember the following and tell an adult:
- What happened?
- Where did it happen?
- When did it happen?
- What did the person look like? How big? How old? Man or woman? Boy or girl? Hair color? Eye color? Skin color? Did the person wear glasses? What kinds of clothing? Any special marks or scars?
- If the person was in a car, what did the car look like? Did the license plate look different from the license plate for your home state? Can you remember the license plate number? Did the car look new or old? Was the car scratched or dented?

Safety with People You Know

Lots of people touch you. Parents hug you. Your brothers and sisters touch you when you play. Your baby sitter may help you get ready for bed. Doctors and dentists touch you when you go for a checkup. Some touches are "good" touches. They do not hurt you or make you feel frightened. However, some touches are "bad" touches. If someone's touch makes you feel uncomfortable or scared, you can say "No!" You can say "No" to adults, even someone you know very well. You can protect your body, especially the parts that are covered by a bathing suit. You can tell a parent, an adult you trust, a teacher, or a doctor, if you have been touched in a way that feels wrong. It is very important to tell someone.

If the first person doesn't believe you, find someone else who will.

ACTivity! Practice what you would say in these situations:

- Your older brother won't stop tickling you, and you don't like it at all.
- Your older sister pinches you very hard.
- A woman you don't know comes up to you on the playground and asks if you will show her the way to the closest grocery store.
- A neighbor invites you into her or his home and offers you some cookies.
- You are separated from your mother at the shopping mall and a woman you don't know offers to help you find her.
- A neighbor says or does something that makes you feel uncomfortable while she or he is taking care of you.

Emergency Who's Who

ACTivity! You can be ready for emergencies. Ask a family member to help you make a list of numbers to keep by the telephone.

Family Work Numbers _____

Neighbor _____

Fire Department _____

Police _____

Ambulance _____

Health Department _____

Poison Control Center _____

Doctor _____

Dentist _____

ACTivity! What would you say or do if you had to make an emergency call? Follow the emergency guide below.

1. Use the emergency list and dial the number you need.
2. Tell who you are. "Hello, my name is _____."
3. Tell where you are. "I am at _____." (Street, apartment, house number, city, state or name of park, trail, building, etc.)
4. Tell what the emergency is. "This is an emergency. I need _____."
5. Try to stay calm and follow directions.

ACTivity! Think of some emergencies and practice making pretend phone calls. One person can be the police or the emergency operator and another person can pretend to make the phone call.

On Your Own at Home

Sometimes you may be at home alone. Know how to make emergency calls, what to do if there is a fire or if the lights go out, and how to answer the phone. This information is good to have, but especially when you are home alone.

Fire Safety

With your family and your Girl Scout group, prepare a plan for what to do in case of fire.

1. Look for anything that can cause a fire indoors or outdoors. Make a list of things to do to reduce the danger of fire.

2. Have a fire drill. Know the best way to get out of your home, especially from the bedrooms. Plan another way to get out if the best exit is blocked by the fire.

3. Remember to drop to the floor and crawl out. The air near the floor is cooler.

ACTivity!

Look at the picture below. Circle all the fire dangers.

What do you do if your clothes catch on fire?

Stop. Do not run or walk or jump around. Moving gives more oxygen to the fire and keeps it going.

Drop. Drop to the ground or floor. Cover your face with your hands.

Roll. Smother the fire by rolling over slowly.

What should you do if another person's clothes catch on fire?

1. Get the person to the ground.
2. Roll her over or use a coat or blanket to smother the flames.
3. Be careful that your own clothing or hair does not catch on fire.

Remember these three words:

Stop

Drop

Roll

Safety in Bad Weather

Thunderstorms

If you hear thunder or see dark clouds, you should follow these safety rules:

- Don't stand in an open field. Crouch down with something between you and the ground. Use a sleeping bag or a pile of clothes, if they are available.

- Don't stand under a tree. Lightning hits tall things first and then travels to the ground. Lightning could hit the tree you are under and you!

- Get out of the water right away. Lightning can strike the water and hurt you.

- Stay out of ditches and arroyos. Storms can turn these ditches into big, fast rivers!

- Get inside a car or indoors. Once you are inside the car, do not touch the metal parts.

- If you are home, close all the windows.

- Don't use the telephone, air conditioner, television, hair dryer, or any other electrical appliance.

Tornadoes

Tornado warnings are usually given on weather reports. If you hear that a tornado is expected where you live, you should follow these safety rules:

- Find shelter. The best places are storm shelters and basements, caves, tunnels, underground parking garages, or the inside hallways of buildings.
- Stay away from windows and outside doorways. Stay away from cars, trailers, tents, school gymnasiums, and auditoriums or stadiums.
- If you cannot find shelter, stay away from the tornado by moving to the side of its path or by lying flat in a ditch, or under a bridge. Put your arms over your head.

When the storm is over:

- Be careful where you walk. Electricity from power lines that have fallen can travel through water and wet ground. If you step in a puddle or on ground that is wet, you can get a big shock!
- Do not go near streams or riverbanks where water is moving quickly. Stay out of ditches and low areas.
- Do not walk on the beach or grass near the ocean. Big waves can move quickly after a storm and come right up onto the beach.

Dressing for the Weather

What do you do if it is raining outside? If it is windy? If it is very sunny? How do you know what the weather will be like? In some places, you can call a weather service. You can also read the weather forecast in a newspaper or listen to the weather report on the radio or on television.

Four types of weather are shown on this page. On the next page, draw pictures of the types of clothes you need for each, or cut out pictures from magazines or catalogs (get permission first) and paste them in the spaces.

Sun Safety Tips

Slip! Slop! Slap! Have fun in the sun!

When you're out in the sun, take care of your skin. Without protection, the sun can give you painful sunburns or blisters. Or make you look old and wrinkly way before your time.

But you can start taking care of your skin now. We call it Sun Basics. And it's as simple as SLIP! SLOP! SLAP! to be safe and have fun in the sun every day!

SLIP! on a shirt.

SLOP! on sunscreen with SPF 15+
    or higher.

SLAP! on a hat.

Now you're ready for fun in the sun!

Sunny Day

Rainy Day

Windy Day

Snowy Day

First Aid

First aid is the first help an injured or sick person receives. It may be washing a cut, saying things to keep someone calm, or getting a doctor.

You should have a first-aid kit in your home, in your family's car, and on Girl Scout outings.

Here are some things to put in the kit:

- First-aid book.
- Soap.
- Safety pins.
- Scissors.
- Tweezers.
- Sewing needle.
- Matches.
- Adhesive tape and sterile gauze dressings.
- Clean cloth.
- Calamine lotion.
- Anti-bacterial antiseptic.
- Emergency telephone numbers.
- Money for phone calls.
- Rubber or plastic gloves.
- Simple face mask.
- Plastic bag.

Infections

A simple cut can be dangerous if it gets infected. This can happen if a cut is not taken care of properly. Signs of infection include swelling, redness, a hot feeling, pain, tenderness, fever, and pus.

If you get a cut, wash your hands with soap and water. Then put on a clean bandage. If you must help someone who has a cut, wear rubber or plastic gloves from your first-aid kit.

Bites and Stings

All bites need first aid because there are lots of bacteria in the mouth. Even small bites can be dangerous. Animal bites can be serious because of infection. Some animals carry rabies, a very dangerous disease. Never go near a wild animal or other animal you do not know. Do not go near an animal you do know if it is acting strangely. If you have been bitten, tell an adult **immediately**. If you know where the animal is, point it out to an adult. If the animal has run away, describe it to an adult.

If you have to help someone who has been bitten, make sure you wear plastic or rubber gloves from your first-aid kit.

Most insect bites are not serious. Your skin may get itchy and swell up a little, but the bite soon goes away—(especially if you do not scratch it! A bee sting can hurt, but usually it is not dangerous. If you get stung by a bee and the stinger is in your skin, try to scrape the stinger out with a clean fingernail or needle. Don't squeeze the stinger. Press a cold washcloth or an ice cube on the sting. If you find a tick on your skin, have an adult help you remove it.

Some people are very allergic to bees and other insects. If they get stung, they may have a hard time breathing. If someone who is allergic gets stung, she must see a doctor or get to a hospital right away.

Burns

A burn is an injury to your skin from heat or chemicals. If you have a burn, run cool water, not ice water, over the burned area. Be gentle with your skin and don't break any blisters (the bubbles of skin) that pop up. Put clean cloth bandages over the burned part. Don't put butter or anything

greasy on it! Find an adult to help you take care of the burn and to decide whether you need to see a doctor or go to a hospital.

Too Much Body Heat

If you stay in the heat or in the bright sun too long, you can get *heat exhaustion* or *heatstroke*.

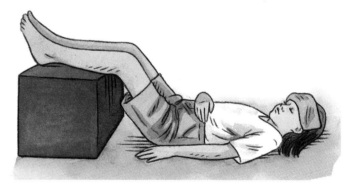

Some signs of heat exhaustion are:
- Feeling weak or feeling like you might throw up.
- Feeling dizzy.
- Bad cramps in your stomach.
- Fainting.
- Skin that feels cool or cold and wet.

Get out of the sun right away and tell and adult that you don't feel well. Put a cool cloth on your forehead and body. Take some sips of water. Lie down and raise your feet. If you don't feel better in an hour, see a doctor. If heat exhaustion is not treated, it can turn into heatstroke.

Heatstroke is very dangerous. It can give you a fever and red hot skin. A person who is suffering from heatstroke needs medical attention fast.

Too Little Body Heat

If you stay outside too long in cold, windy, or wet weather, you can get *hypothermia*. Wearing the right clothes and a hat is very important. Hypothermia can make you shiver, your teeth chatter, your hands and feet feel cold. You need to get inside right away and slowly eat or drink something that is warm.

Frostbite

When it is very cold, the parts of your body that are not protected can actually freeze. This is called *frostbite*. Most

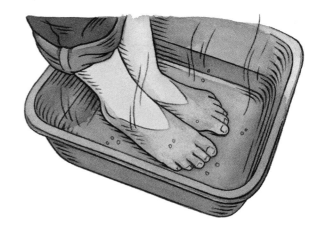

frostbite happens in the fingers, toes, nose, cheeks, and ears. The skin may be slightly red and then turn white or grayish-yellow. There is no pain in the frost-bitten part. You can get blisters and your skin will still feel cold and numb. Frostbite is dangerous. Find an adult to help. Go indoors and warm up. Don't rub the skin. Put the frost-bitten part of your body in warm (not hot) water, or gently wrap it with a sheet and warm blankets. See a doctor right away.

Nosebleeds

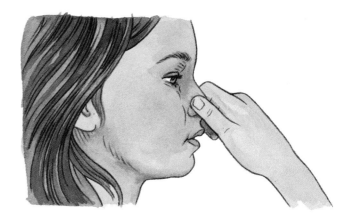

Nosebleeds can happen when the air is very dry, if you have had a cold, if you are in a very high place, like the mountains, or if you hurt your nose. Try to stop the bleeding by sitting down and squeezing your nose firmly for about 10 minutes or until the bleeding stops. Placing cold towels on your nose may help. If the bleeding continues, get an adult to help you.

Bumps and Bruises

Put a damp, cold cloth on the area. If there is a lot of swelling, ask an adult to help you.

Choking

If the person can speak, cough, and breathe, do nothing. Otherwise, stand behind the person and grasp your hands around her, just under her rib cage. Press your hands into her stomach with four quick upward moves. Do this until the person spits out the food or object.

If you are choking, move your hand across your throat to let others know. If no one is around, try pressing your hands into your stomach with four quick upward moves. Or quickly press your stomach into a chair back to try to release the object.

Poisoning

This is always serious and a big emergency. If you or someone you know has swallowed poison, call the poison control center and your emergency first-aid number immediately. Many things in your home can poison you if you swallow them. Bleach, furniture polish, and nail polish remover are just a few of them.

Don't ever take any kinds of medications, drugs, or pills unless they have been prescribed for you by a doctor and an adult is present.

Brownie Girl Scouts need to keep their bodies and minds healthy so they can enjoy the zillions of activities and adventures awaiting them this year and next and on into becoming Junior, Cadette, and Senior Girl Scouts.

Books You Might Like to Read

Cohen, Miriam. *Welcome to First Grade.*
New York: Bantam Doubleday Dell, 1998.

Dr. Seuss. *Oh the Places You'll Go.*
New York: Random House, 1990.

Freeman, Don. *Dandelion.*
New York: Puffin, 1987.

Goble, Paul. *The Girl Who Loved
Wild Horses.* Fort Worth: Aladdin
Publishing, 1993.

Martin, Rafe. *The Brave Little Parrot.*
New York: Putnam, 1998.

McCloskey, Robert. *One Morning in Maine.*
New York: Viking Press, 1952.

Roop, Peter, and Connie Roop.
Keep the Lights Burning, Abbie.
Minneapolis: Carolrhoda Books, 1992.

Williamson, Sarah A. *Stop, Look, and
Listen: Using Your Senses from Head to Toe.*
Charlotte, Vt.: Williamson Publishing, 1996.

Chapter

3

FAMILY AND FRIENDS

Family and Friends

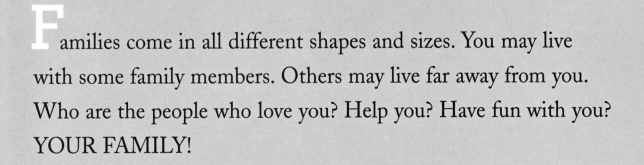

Families come in all different shapes and sizes. You may live with some family members. Others may live far away from you. Who are the people who love you? Help you? Have fun with you? YOUR FAMILY!

What Makes Up a Family?

ACTivity! Hidden in this puzzle are 18 words that have something to do with families: smile, adult, love, youngsters, family, giggles, joke, hugs, songs, home, rules, meals, play, learn, manners, trips, fun, and YOU! The words are across, diagonal, and up and down! How many can you find? For the answers, see page 88 in this book.

M	E	P	L	A	Y	L	E	A	R	N
E	Y	O	U	N	G	S	T	E	R	S
A	S	F	U	N	U	Q	X	C	B	J
L	G	W	A	D	T	R	I	P	S	H
S	U	Z	D	M	A	N	N	E	R	S
H	H	W	U	G	I	G	G	L	E	S
W	E	B	L	R	U	L	E	S	J	O
V	P	L	T	S	X	O	Y	H	O	N
H	O	M	E	A	V	V	O	K	K	G
X	D	S	M	I	L	E	U	T	E	S

Making Memories

ACTivity! Make a "Me and My Family" album. You can use words, pictures from magazines, drawings, and photographs. Include things that are important to you and your family members (or show them in some way), like:

- Sayings.
- Dates such as birthdays, anniversaries, or the day you got your first pet.
- Meals and recipes.
- Events like soccer games, ballet recitals, piano concerts, or a Brownie Girl Scout ceremony.
- Favorite movies or videos.
- Favorite songs.
- Religious practices.

To: Mom
From: Alice

Have A Happy Thanks- -giving

ADMIT ONE
985003

Growing Strong Families

Have you ever taken care of a plant or worked in a garden? If so, you know that for a plant to grow tall and strong, it needs water, light, and soil. Just like that plant, families need special care and feeding, too! In order to grow a healthy, happy family, you need to do things together and help each other.

Family Fun

Everyone likes to do fun things. And doing them together helps your family feel close to each other. Do you need some ideas? Here are five fun-tastic ones to try!

1. R.S.V.P.

(French for "respondez s'il vous plait," which means "Please respond.") Invite your family to share a meal together.

- Make invitations.
- Deliver them to your family members.
- With an adult, plan a meal that will be easy to prepare and serve.
- Ask everyone to answer one question. (You might ask, "What did you learn today?" or "What is your favorite thing to do and why?") Listen to what each person says.

2. Take a Hike

Step out with your family! Walking is great exercise. And it's easy, too. You could hike through a park or a nature center. Or you could just walk around your neighborhood. Make a game of it. Look around you while you're hiking. Who can identify the types of trees? Flowers? Rocks? Who takes the longest steps? Who is the fastest walker? No running!

3. Game Night

Make one night "Game Night." Play card games, board games, word games, or acting games. Or try more active games like tag, softball, or soccer!

Find new ways to celebrate. Turn a regular party into something special by making incredible decorations or keeping it a surprise. But you don't need a party to celebrate. Instead, you can:

- Exchange friendship bracelets.
- Recite a poem together.
- Sing a song about the event.
- Say a prayer.
- Help others.

For more ideas, look through this book or *Try-Its for Brownie Girl Scouts* with your family. Maybe a game, science activity, crafts, or math challenge will grab your family's attention. Or plan an event with your Girl Scout troop or group that celebrates families. If you share your Girl Scouting activities with your family, everyone can enjoy them!

4. Learn a Skill

Everyone has a special talent. Is your dad a great cook? Does your sister design terrific-looking Web sites? Is your brother an awesome artist? Each one gets a turn to teach her or his special skill to the rest of the family.

5. Make It Special

Every family has events they celebrate: birthdays, holidays, and anniversaries. Families often celebrate the same event year after year. In this way, a family's tradition develops.

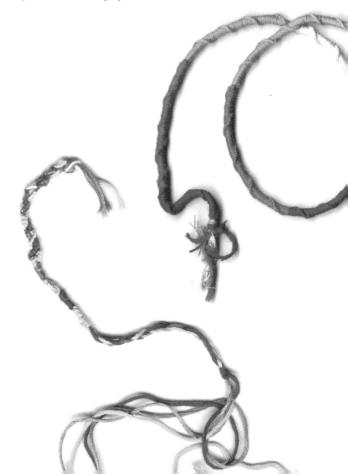

Family Differences

Your brothers and sisters may go to the same school, eat the same meals, and maybe even sleep in the same room as you. They know you pretty well. This means they know how to make you laugh. But it also means they know how to make you cry. It might seem like they are your best friends one minute and your enemies the next. Learning to get along with your brothers or sisters can be hard. But feeling close to them is worth it!

DO's and DON'Ts to Succeed with Your Brothers and Sisters

- DON'T go into your sibling's room if he or she is not there. (A sibling is a brother or sister.)
- DO knock before entering. Everyone needs some privacy.
- DO set time aside to play with them – give them some attention and they'll give you some peace.
- DON'T pester them if they want to be alone.
- DON'T take or wear their things without asking.
- DO make sure that you return what you've borrowed in good condition.
- DO tell a grown-up if you think a brother or sister is in trouble or could get hurt.

Nothing is more important than family. Treat your siblings as well as you'd treat your best friend. And who knows? You just might find out that they are!

Friends

Friends are very special. A friend may be just like you or very different. Friends play, share, and go places with each other.

Fantastic People,

Reliable Pals,

It's Fun to Share

Exciting Times.

Never Dull When

Do You Have

Special Friends

ACTivity! You can make a poem like this using a friend's name or by using your own. Try it!

Finding Friends

Where can you find friends? Almost everywhere! Keep your eyes open in your neighborhood, at school, camp, and your place of worship. Lots of times friends share an interest like sports or drawing. Introduce yourself to the other girls and boys you meet at art class or softball practice. When you become friendly, ask what other activities they like. Share what you like. You'll find that friends can be alike in some ways and different in many others. Sometimes the differences can make it more fun to be together.

In fact, by trying what your friend likes, you may discover that you like it, too. She might introduce you to hiking and you might teach her the butterfly stroke.

Be patient. Friendships take time to grow. Girl Scouts is a great place to make friends because you can spend time with each other. Together you can learn new things, try new activities, share silly jokes, and go places. Work together on a Try-It activity.

Friends at School

You might meet some of your best friends at school. After all, the girls and boys in your class will be your own age and some may even live in the neighborhood. Maybe you can walk home or take the bus together, do your homework together, or even have a sleep over.

Usually, you and your friends at school will get along. But sometimes you might have a fight that upsets you. If you and your classmate can't work it out on your own, talk to your teacher. While your teacher's most important job is to help you learn about reading, writing, and arithmetic, she can also help you to solve problems with other kids. Maybe she can help the two of you talk about it. Or maybe she can just listen to what is making you feel bad and help you to find other ways of looking at the problem. If your classmates are teasing or insulting you, she can ask them to stop.

At school there may be bigger or older kids who try to scare you or to make you do things that you do not want to do. They might try to do mean things like take your lunch money or scribble in your books. These kids are bullies. Learn how to stand up for yourself. The best idea is to first tell them no in a loud, clear voice. If that doesn't work, talk to your teachers and your parents or guardians. Usually, bullies are trying to make themselves feel good by making someone else feel bad. If you stand up for yourself, you won't give them a chance to feel good and maybe they will leave you alone.

Lisa,

I hope you are in
my class next year!

Love, Heather

Being a Good Friend

To have a friend, you have to be a friend.

How good a friend are **you**? Look at the list below. What else can you do to be a good friend?

1. HAVE FUN TOGETHER!

Plan to do fun stuff with your friends. Try something different if you are not in the mood for adventure.

2. BE CARING.

Hurt feelings are painful. To avoid hurting your friends, be sure you don't tease them. If you do, stop and apologize.

3. SHARE.

Sharing involves lots more than just your toys. Sometimes you might have to share your mom's or your Girl Scout leader's attention. At times, you might have to share your space, your bedroom, or the back seat of the car. But when you share with your friends, they will also share with you.

4. BE LOYAL.

Stick up for your friend when someone else is being mean. Also, don't talk about her behind her back.

Faraway Friends

A friend moves out of town. It's the last day of camp. You start classes at a new school. That doesn't mean your friendships are over. You can stay in touch in so many ways. You can:

- Be pen pals. Send letters, e-mail, note cards, photos, or postcards to each other. Create and send drawings and other artwork.
- Send a story. Start writing a story. After a few sentences, send her what you've written. Ask her to write the next couple of lines and send it back to you. How long can you keep the story going? How silly can you make it? How scary? Try adding some illustrations to your story.

Friends with Other Abilities

Everyone has different abilities. Some people have physical problems that cause them to use eyeglasses, hearing aids, or wheelchairs. Some people have illnesses that force them to take medicine. Other people find it hard to learn or pay attention. No matter how a person looks or acts, everyone has feelings and likes to have friends who treat her with respect.

Some children have learning disabilities. That means that there is something in the way the brain gets information that makes it harder to learn. One child may see things backwards. Another may see letters in different ways each time she reads them. Girls who have these kinds of disabilities may need special material or instruction. Remember that a girl with a disability can still be a great friend and a talented student.

Consider someone who cannot hear perfectly, or even at all. She may need you to speak more loudly or to stand where she can see your lips move. Or she may need you to repeat your ideas. Mostly, she will need you to be patient. In this situation, you could even learn the sign language finger alphabet below. Try it. Or you could learn American Sign Language. *ACTivity!*

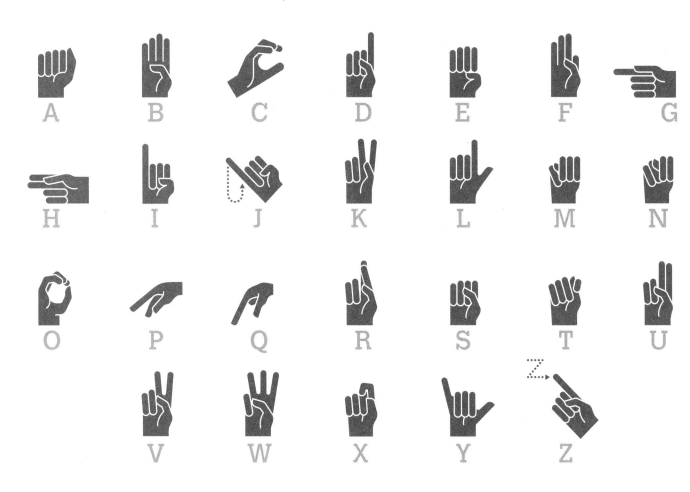

When Friendships Fade

Some friendships last forever. Others don't. When a friendship ends, it doesn't mean that either of you has done something wrong. Friendships end for lots of reasons:

- Changing interests. Maybe you've become very involved in an acting group, and your friend is on three sports teams, leaving you with little time to see one another.
- Moving. Sometimes, no matter how hard you try to stay in touch, a friendship does not survive a move. It's hard to continue to feel close to a friend you never see.

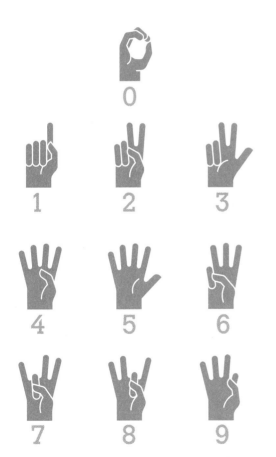

Getting Along

No matter how close friends are, sometimes they have fights. So do families. Have you done any of these?

1 Teasing. It may seem funny to others, but the person who's being teased is not laughing.

2 Spending too little time with your friend. Friends need to spend time together to keep their friendship strong.

3 Spreading gossip. If a friend has shared a secret with you, keep it a secret. You'd want her to keep your secrets, right? If the secret is about someone who's hurt or might be harmed in some way, always tell an adult you trust.

4 Not sharing your friends. Are you insisting that she be only your friend? If you make her choose, she may choose the other girl.

5 Being bossy. Do you tell your friend what to do? Would you want a friend like that?

You and your friend want to play different games. But you only have time to play one game. Compromise is the answer. Compromise involves each of you letting go of some of what you want to reach a happy solution. Maybe play one game today and the other one tomorrow.

Books You Might Like to Read

Friends

Brown, Laurie K. *How to Be a Friend.*
Boston: Little, Brown and Co., 1998.

Pleasant Company. *The Care and Feeding
of Friends.* Middleton, Wis.:
Pleasant Company, 1998.

———.
Games and Giggles. Middleton, Wis.:
Pleasant Company, 1998.

———.
More Games and Giggles. Middleton, Wis.:
Pleasant Company, 1998.

Steiner, Joan. *Look-Alikes.*
Boston: Little, Brown and Co., 1998.

Viorst, Judith. *Rosie and Michael.*
New York: Simon & Schuster, 1974.

Family

Kroll, Virginia L. *Beginnings: How Families
Come to Be.* New York: Concept Books,
1994.

Polacco, Patricia. *Thundercake.*
New York: Philomel Books, 1990.

Ringgold, Faith. *Tar Beach.*
Albuquerque, N.Mex.: Dragonfly, 1996.

Sweeney, Joan. *Me and My Family Tree.*
Santa Clara, Calif.: Crown Publishers, 1999.

Viorst, Judith. *I'll Fix Anthony.*
New York: Simon & Schuster, 1998.

Wilhelm, Hans. *I'll Always Love You.*
Santa Clara, Calif.: Crown, 1985.

Answers to word puzzle on page 78.

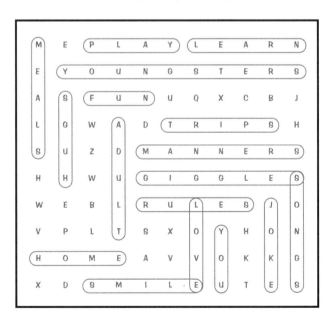

WHAT'S OUT THERE?

What's Out There?

You live in a home, no matter if it's a houseboat, house, apartment, trailer, or teepee! Outside your home there is a neighborhood—people, businesses, schools, parks, and things like that! Beyond your neighborhood there is a town, city, state, country, and even the world. Whether you know it or not, you are a member of all these communities. And your actions can be important in all of them.

Your Home

Your home is the place where you live, eat, and sleep. There are many different types of homes. Describe your home. What do you like best about it? Can you think of a story about your home? Share it with another Brownie Girl Scout or a friend.

Your Neighborhood

Your neighborhood is the area close to your home. It is made up of people, places, and things. Maps can help you become familiar with your neighborhood. Ask an adult to show you a map that you might use to get from your troop's meeting place to a zoo, library, or your favorite pizza place. Your map may have symbols. Ask how to use the symbols that appear on the map.

ACTivity! Draw a map of one part of your neighborhood. Include your school, a garden, a stable, Mrs. Wilson sitting on her front porch, or even your dentist's office.

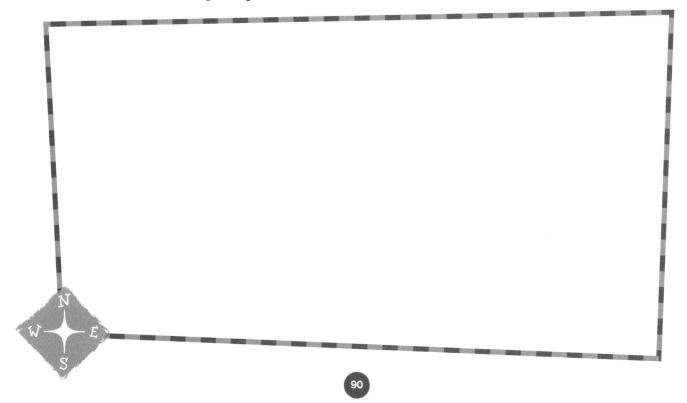

Your Community

A community is a group of people who live in the same area. Your neighborhood is a part of your community. So is your Girl Scout troop!

The people in your community will not all look the same. There may be young people and old people. There may be short and tall people. There may be people with dark skin and with light skin.

People also have different religions. Some will go to a temple. Some will go to a church. Some will go to a synagogue or another place of worship.

Learn more about the people in your community by holding a holiday celebration with your Brownie Girl Scout troop. Each girl can share a favorite food, decoration, or song. Maybe a girl would like to share a special story about her family's history.

Changes in Your Community

Chances are that your community did not always look the same. Changes like more streets, fewer open spaces, more businesses, and bigger buildings may have taken place.

Ask your parents about changes they remember. Ask an elderly person about how your neighborhood looked a long time ago. Keep notes about what they say. Compare your notes with the notes of other girls in your troop. Using all the information that you have collected as a troop, build a model of the community as it appeared long ago. When your model is done, write a story about what it was like to live in the neighborhood way back then. Invite those people who shared their memories to hear you read your story.

Sharing and Caring

Girl Scouts are an important part of the community. A Girl Scout service project helps the people in the community in some way. Look around your neighborhood. Do you see something that might be a problem? Can you think of how to fix the problem? Talk about this with your troop and your leader.

Answering the following questions will start you on the way to completing a service project.

1. What do you want to do? Help the environment? Help hungry people?
2. What do you need? Materials? More girls?
3. How long do you think it will take to finish your project? Four days? Two weeks? A month?
4. Who will help you? Another troop? Your leader? Your parents?
5. What should you do first? Second? Make a plan.

Here are some ideas for service projects:

• Plant flowers at a public building or in a special place in your community. Keep that spot beautiful for everyone to enjoy. First ask for permission to plant your flowers.

• Collect canned cat and dog food, old towels and blankets, pet toys, and newspapers for a local animal shelter.

• Make Valentine cards for senior citizens in a nursing home or community center. Present the cards and sing songs about love on Valentine's Day.

Your Environment

The environment is made up of air, land, water, plants, and animals. Both living and nonliving things are part of your environment.

How can you tell if something is alive or not? Here are some clues:

• Is it breathing?
• Does it need water?
• Does it make or get its own food?
• Does it grow?
• Does it die?

If you answered yes to at least two of these questions, the thing is alive.

ACTivity! Write down some of the things in your environment that are alive and some that are not.

Alive

_____

_____

_____

Not Alive

_____

_____

_____

The Weather Outside Is...

Weather is the condition of the air outside at a certain time in a certain place. Is the weather cold, wet, or windy today? Or is it sunny and warm?

When people describe how the weather usually is in a certain area, they are talking about the *climate*. If a city is described as being tropical, the climate is warm and wet.

Keeping Track of the Weather

Be a weather watcher. Get a large calendar. Make sure that it has boxes for the days of the week. Draw a symbol for the weather on the box for each day for a month. What would you draw to show a sunny day? A rainy day? Cloudy? Windy? Lots of fog? Snow?

Weather Watch Hunt

ACTivity! Go for a walk outside and look for the things described in the list below. When you find something on the list, check it off.

- Something warmed by the sun.
- Something in the shade.
- A place that is cool.
- A place that is hot.
- Something blowing in the wind.
- Something left by the rain.
- Something wet by the rain.
- Something that will protect you from the rain.
- A cloud shaped like an animal.
- An object with icicles on it.
- A snowdrift.
- An object hidden by snow.
- A good place to go in case of a hurricane.
- A good place to go in case of a tornado.
- A place to protect you from the wind.
- An animal that seems to be enjoying the weather.

Make your own list of weather watch items. Give the list to someone else.

Measuring Rain

ACTivity! How do the weather people on television or radio know how much rain fell from the sky? They get their information from places called weather stations, where rain gauges are set up. A rain gauge measures the amount of rain that falls.

You can make a simple rain gauge. You will need a clear glass jar with straight sides and a flat bottom and a ruler. Make sure the opening is as wide as the sides of the jar.

Just before a rainstorm, place your jar outside in an open area with no trees. After the rain has stopped, hold a ruler to the side of your gauge. How high is the water in the jar? Do the same thing every day for a week, or even a month. (Be sure to use the same jar.) What did you find out?

The weather and the soil type determine the kinds of plants that will grow in a particular place. If it is very rainy and warm and there is rich soil, many different types of plants will grow. And they'll grow quickly.

Looking at Plants

Plants like trees and flowers are all around you. They make oxygen for you to breathe. Trees provide shade. Flowers are beautiful to look at. Some are sweet smelling. Many plants provide people with food. Can you think of some?

Plant Parts Scramble

ACTivity! See how much you know about the parts of a plant. Try to unscramble the words below.

1. MTSE
I hold up the plant. This makes sure that the leaves and flowers reach the sunlight.
    Which part am I? _____

2. ROWLFE
I am a colorful part where the plant makes its seeds. I have petals.
    Which part am I? _____

3. TORO
I slurp up water and minerals from the soil. I also hold the plant in place.
    Which part am I? _____

4. AFLE
I make food for the plant from air, water, and sunlight.
    Which part am I? _____

5. DESE
I am the part with a hard outer covering. A baby plant is inside of me.
    Which part am I? _____

    Plants need water, sunlight, minerals from the soil, air, and space to grow. They grow faster in warm weather.

How Do Plants Drink?

ACTivity! Try this experiment. You will need a piece of celery with leaves on it, a glass of water, and red or blue food coloring.

Put 3 to 4 drops of red or blue food coloring in the glass of water. Cut a small piece off the bottom of the celery. Place it in the glass of water. Wait a few hours. What happens?

You will see the color move up the celery's stalk to the leaves. A plant loses water through its leaves. The roots must take in more water. The water moves up the stem of a plant to the leaves.

Cut another small piece off the bottom of the piece of celery. You will see colored spots. These are the ends of the thin tubes that the water moves through.

Seed Hunt

⚠ Many plants make seeds, and new plants grow from some of these seeds. Go on a seed hunt and collect a bunch of different kinds of seeds. Before you go, make sure you know what poison ivy looks like so that you can avoid it. Even the seeds can give you a rash.

Study the shapes of the seeds you have found. Ask yourself how they move around. They don't have legs or feet. They can't run or walk. For example, you find a seed that has small spikes or hooks. How do you think it would get around? Who might carry it away? If you guessed "animals," you would be right. The seeds stick to the fur of creatures like deer, raccoons, foxes, mice, skunks, and rabbits. They even stick to people's clothes! Many seeds are also carried away by the wind.

Did you find a seed that looks like it has wings? That's a maple seed. Throw it up in the air to see what happens.

Return all the seeds you have looked at to where you found them.

Understanding Animals

Many people have pets at home—dogs, cats, rabbits, birds, hamsters, or guinea pigs. Do you have a pet?

Your pet probably enjoys when you play with it, give it a treat, or scratch behind its ears. But if you love your pet, there are some things you should never do to it.

ACTivity!

My Pet Pledge

I will always treat my pet with love

   and understanding

I will leave my pet alone when it is eating

I will not bother my pet when it is sleeping

I will always be gentle when touching my pet

I will make sure my pet gets exercise

I will make sure my pet has fresh food and water

Your Name _____

Some Pet Safety Tips to Remember

1. Don't stare eye to eye—many animals, especially dogs, can take this as a signal to fight.

2. Don't surprise a sleeping pet—it might overreact, even bite, before realizing that it's you.

3. Remember, pets can get grumpy. If your pet is acting like it wants to be left alone, respect that.

4. Many animals don't like to have anyone near them while they are eating. Do not touch your pet when it is eating.

Dog Smarts Quiz

ACTivity! It is also important to respect other people's pets. When you see dogs in your neighborhood, how should you behave? Take the quiz below and see how much you already know. Answer either true or false to each question.

1. I should try to pet dogs that are behind fences or tied up in backyards.
   True or false? _____

2. I should stand very still and be quiet if a strange dog without a leash comes up to me.
   True or false? _____

3. If I see someone walking a dog on a leash, I should ask permission to pet the dog.
   True or false? _____

4. If an owner gives me permission to pet a dog, I should first let the dog smell my closed hand.
   True or false? _____

5. I should chase any loose dogs that I see in my neighborhood.
   True or false? _____

6. A dog wagging its tail always means it's friendly.
   True or false? _____

Answers: 1—false; 2—true; 3—true; 4—true; 5—false; 6—false

What's in a Habitat?

Plants, animals, and nonliving things are all part of a *habitat*. A habitat is a place where an animal or plant lives. It is like the animal's or plant's address. It is where an animal or plant finds the food, water, shelter, and space it needs to survive.

Hanging Around in a Habitat

ACTivity! With your troop, explore a habitat near you. It could be a park, a forest, a field, or a pond. Collect a few things that you find on the ground to make a habitat mobile.

Note: You don't want to harm the habitat you are studying. Do not pick flowers or break off living tree branches. Instead, collect dead branches and twigs from the ground for your mobile. Another idea is to use an old coat hanger and some pencils.

Did you find any nonliving things? How about rocks or pebbles?

Think of ideas for materials to use to show which plants are found in your habitat.

Did you find something to represent an animal? A leaf with chew marks made by insects? If not, draw a picture of an animal that lives in your habitat or cut out some photos from old magazines.

You will need some string or thread to make your mobile. Now follow these steps:

1. With the string, tie the smaller twigs (or pencils) to the larger branch (the coat hanger). See the picture below.

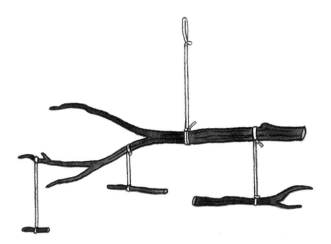

2. Wrap some string around each habitat piece.
3. Choose a place in the mobile to tie the piece.

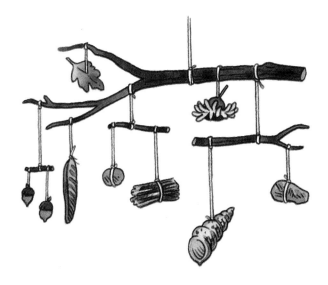

4. Find a special place to display your mobile!

Aiding the Environment

To *conserve* means to save something from loss or waste. When you write or draw on both sides of the paper, you are conserving. If you put your aluminum cans or old newspapers out to be recycled, this is also conserving. Conserving in nature is particularly important because there are only so many trees and so much clean water and air.

Both people and animals need natural resources to survive. Many times, the homes of wild animals are destroyed or changed because people move into their environments and forget to conserve what already exists there. Sometimes destroying just a small part of a habitat will mean that an animal can no longer live there. These animals can become endangered unless people take great care to put the habitat and environment back in order.

Pollution Police

What is pollution and what can you do about it? Pollution is anything that damages the air, water, and soil. You have the power to help stop pollution. Always put your litter in a garbage can. Never just drop it on the ground. "Pack out" all the remains of the food and wrappings that you take with you on a hike, leaving nothing at all on the trail.

One way to fight air pollution is to plant trees. Trees take in polluted air and release oxygen. People and other living things need oxygen to breathe. Planting a tree may be a good activity for an Earth Day celebration.

What are some other things that you can do to stop polluting? How can you help adults think about pollution and take steps toward eliminating it and improving the environment?

Water, Water Everywhere

Most of the earth is covered with water. But fresh water is an extremely important resource. In some parts of the world it is very difficult to get clean water. Some people must make one bucketful last for an entire day. That bucket of water may have to be used to wash, clean, cook, and drink.

Do you know how much water you use? Keep track of all the ways that you use water in one day. Think of ways that you can conserve water.

Taking Out the Garbage

Garbage is a big pollution problem. One answer is not to make too much of it. Here are some ideas for cutting down on garbage:

- Make rags out of your old, stained, or torn clothes. Use them instead of paper towels to clean up around the house.
- Save plastic and paper shopping bags. Use them to carry your lunch or to make book covers.
- Return plastic and paper to recycling centers. Some recycled materials are reused to make containers or cardboard boxes.

Make a Recycled Bird Feeder

ACTivity! You will need a plastic gallon milk container, scissors, a ruler, bird food, wire, and string.

1. Wash the container. Measure two inches up from the bottom of the container. With the scissors, cut up through the middle of one side of the milk container and make a large hole.

2. Tie the string around the handle of the milk container. Make a hole in the cap and attach the string or wire. Place bird food (seeds, suet, peanut butter) in the bottom two inches of the container.

3. Hang your feeder from the branch of a tree. How many kinds of birds visit your feeder? Try putting out different types of seed (sunflower, millet, cracked corn, safflower). Do certain birds like certain types of seed?

Make a Recycled Work of Art

Collect junk mail, magazines, newspapers, wrapping paper, cardboard paper rolls, egg cartons, cardboard boxes, items made from aluminum foil, plastic bottles, bottle caps, margarine tubs, etc.

With friends, see who can recycle the materials into something usable, pretty, or funny. You may need a stapler, glue, and tape. Use your imagination! Display your work of art.

Working for the Environment

Do you like to plant trees or watch birds? Maybe you would like to be the person to find new ways to clean up oil spills. There are many different jobs that have to do with the environment. A forester, for example, protects trees and decides how to use forests to make products for people. An oceanographer studies the oceans and the plants and animals that live in them.

Your First Adventures

ACTivity! Your first trip as a Girl Scout doesn't need to be far from home. Look around your community. Which places would you like to visit? Write the names of those places here.

....

....

....

....

....

....

....

....

Carry a small pad and a pencil or two when you go on a trip or even when you go out in the neighborhood. Draw or write what you see on the pad. Maybe you'll want to make a troop scrapbook about your trip.

Before your trip, pick a buddy. Stay with your buddy at all times. You and your buddy must make sure to stay with your leader, or the other adults, during the trip. If you get separated from your troop, stay where you are.

Fill out the diary below after you have come back from your trip as a way of remembering the fun you had that day!

Your Girl Scout Trip Diary ACTivity!

Your name ....

Date of trip ....

Name of place you visited ....

How did you get there? ....

Did you like this place? Why? ....

....

....

What was your favorite thing about the place? ....

....

....

What didn't you like? ....

....

....

Why? ....

....

....

Would you like to visit this place again?　　Q yes　　Q no

Which other place(s) would you like to visit? ....

....

....

....

Books Are Great!

Visit a library in your community. You can learn more about weather or a famous woman like Harriet Tubman. Ask the librarian to show you how to look up subjects you are curious to know more about. You'll need a library card to borrow a book. If you don't already have a library card, find out how to get one. Take a book home to read. Don't forget to return it to the library on time!

Do you like to read aloud? Choose a poem, a short story, or a part of one of your favorite books to read aloud to younger children during story time at the library.

Make up your own story and tell it to the members of your troop. You can also tell a real-life story about something that happened to you or a friend or a member of your family.

At the Zoo

Would you like to visit places where you can see plants and animals? Name a few. Did you come up with zoos, gardens, parks, aquariums and nature centers? Plan to visit one of these places. Some of them may be far away from where you live.

When you visit the zoo, read any signs that you see in front of an exhibit for information about the animals. Stand quietly for a few minutes. Watch the animals closely. You may catch them playing with each other, eating, or snuggling with a parent.

Find an animal at the zoo to write a cinquain poem about. A cinquain poem has five lines, as in this example:

Tiger
Striped, strong
Swimming, running, sleeping
With big teeth and claws
Powerful

ACTivity!

To write a cinquain poem of your own:
1. Use one word to name the subject.
2. Use two words to describe the subject (like "strong" or "big").
3. Write three action words about the subject (words ending with "ing").
4. Use a four- or five-word phrase about the subject. (A phrase can start with "like a …" or "with a …" or "full of…." It is not a complete sentence.)
5. Write a final word that sums up how you see the animal.

....

....

....

....

....

In the Park

In some parks, you can go swimming, boating, or horseback riding. Some parks are places of natural beauty with ponds, trees, and flowers. Take a trip to a local or state park. Here are some fun things you can do.

- Sit back-to-back on the ground with a friend. Pick up a fallen leaf or look at a nearby flower and describe it carefully to your friend. Ask your friend to guess what it is that you are describing.

- Be a plant detective. Study the shapes of leaves on different plants. Are the leaves the same shape or different from one plant to another? Sketch the shapes on your pad. How many different shapes did you draw?

- Learn how to use a pair of binoculars and become a bird watcher. See how many birds you can spot. Are they all the same color? Where do you see them? On the ground? In the trees? In the air?

Getting Ready for the Outdoors

Camping Adventures

As a Girl Scout, your first overnight outdoor adventure may be with your troop in a tent in your backyard, the local park, or at a Girl Scout camp.

When you go camping, you might plan to hike, tie knots, or do crafts. You can earn a Try-It while learning about the stars, the weather, or the animals and plants. You can plan ceremonies, games, and parties.

Planning Ahead for Camping

Everyone in your troop will have ideas about what to do on a camping trip. There will be more ideas than you can put into action in one trip. To make sure that everyone has a good time, it's important to plan. Start by writing everyone's ideas on a large sheet of paper. Then, let every girl check off what:

• She wants to do most of all.
• She might want to do if there is time.
• She does not want to do at all.

When you are finished, your chart might look like the one on this page.

PLANNING CHART

What I want to do at camp	Most of all	If there is time	Not at all
Sleep in a cabin	☐	☐	☐
Sleep in a tent	☐	☐	☐
Go on a hike	☐	☐	☐
Go fishing	☐	☐	☐
Learn new songs	☐	☐	☐
Find out about the stars	☐	☐	☐
Do crafts	☐	☐	☐
Discover what animals live at camp	☐	☐	☐
Learn to use a compass	☐	☐	☐
Play games and sports	☐	☐	☐

What to Wear

What is it like where you are going on your trip? What do you need to know before starting out? Learn how to choose the best clothing for different kinds of weather and activities. Here are some clothing tips:

- Wear comfortable shoes and socks for long walks or hikes. Never wear new shoes.
- On a hot day, wear loose clothing. It lets air move in and out around your body. Pick clothes made of cotton. Cotton lets your body heat escape and helps you feel cool. Light colors are cooler than dark ones.

- On a cold day, wear layers of clothing to hold your body heat better. Wool keeps you warm in cold weather because it helps keep your body heat close to you. Always wear a hat.

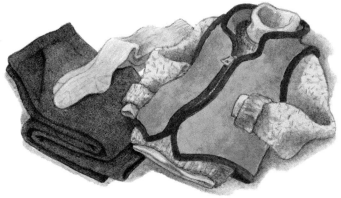

- Wear a hat with a brim when hiking on sunny days. In cold, windy weather, wear a wool hat to keep you warm.

- Protect against sunburn. In sunny weather, wear a hat and a light, cotton, long-sleeved shirt when walking. No matter what the weather, put on sunscreen lotion that has a sun protection factor (SPF) of 15 or higher. You can find the number on the lotion container.

What to Pack

Now you have to pack for your overnight camping trip. Think before you pack. You will have to carry everything that you take with you.

The list below will give you ideas about what to pack—you surely won't need everything it includes. What you pack will depend on the weather during the time of year you are going camping. Are you sleeping outside or in a cabin? Your leader or the other adults will bring the tents, cooking equipment, and food supplies, or they will be available at your campsite.

My Personal Overnight Kit

Warm Weather Clothes
___underwear
___long pants (cotton)
___shorts
___T-shirts
___long-sleeved shirts
___sweaters/sweatshirts
___socks
___sun hat
___bathing suit
___sneakers

Cold Weather Clothes
___hat
___gloves
___warm jacket
___long underwear
___warm boots
___thick socks

Wet Weather Clothes
___water repellent jacket/poncho
___waterproof boots

Sleeping and Eating Gear
___sleeping bag/bedroll
___ground pad
___water bottle
___mess kit (plate cup, bowl, spoon, fork, knife)
___sleepwear
___flashlight with extra bulbs and batteries
___duffel bag/backpack

Other Gear
___comfortable shoes/hiking boots
___bandannas
___daypack
___sit-upon
___whistle (for emergencies)

Personal Items
___soap and shampoo
___towel
___washcloth
___toothbrush/toothpaste
___comb/brush
___sunscreen
___lip balm

Some Hiking Tips

Whenever you hike, always bring a full water bottle. Drink plenty of water, especially when it's hot. If you get lost on a hike, stay where you are. Blow your whistle and wait for help.

You should also carry along some food. Use this recipe to mix up some gorp before your camping trip. Make up a few plastic sandwich bags of gorp to take along on any hikes.

ACTivity! Here is a recipe:

- 2 cups of dry cereal.
- 1 cup of raisins.
- 1 cup of dried fruit (banana chips, apricots, apples, etc.).
- 1 cup of nuts (whichever you like).
- 1 cup of chocolate chips.

Making Knots

Practice tying a few simple knots before you go on a camping trip. This will help you wrap up your sleeping bag and other gear. Besides, it's a great skill to have!

An *overhand knot* is a knot in the end of a rope. This knot is made with one piece of rope. Follow the steps in the picture.

A *square knot* is used to tie two ropes together or to tie a package. It is also the knot used to tie a bandanna around your neck. Tie two pieces of rope together, following the steps in the picture. Remember this poem: "Right over left and left over right makes the knot neat and tidy and tight."

Fun Things to Do at Camp

Make Animal Tracks

Together with your leader and the other girls, go on a detective hike around your camp area. Try to spot any mysterious footprints or animal tracks from creatures big and small. After you have found some prints, try the following activity.

Mix the plaster of Paris (that your leader has brought along) and water by following the directions on the package. Wait 10 minutes until the plaster begins to thicken. Pour it over the track or prints and let it harden for one hour. Lift the plaster and brush away the dirt. You have you very own animal footprint!

Create Pine Cone Art

Each girl will need to gather one pine cone. (If there are no pine cones in your part of the country, use the cones from alder or fir trees.) Try to find cones that have already lost their seeds. Don't take away too many cones that have seeds. Remember that trees grow from seeds.

Create a creature from your pine cone. Use your imagination!

My Treasure Map

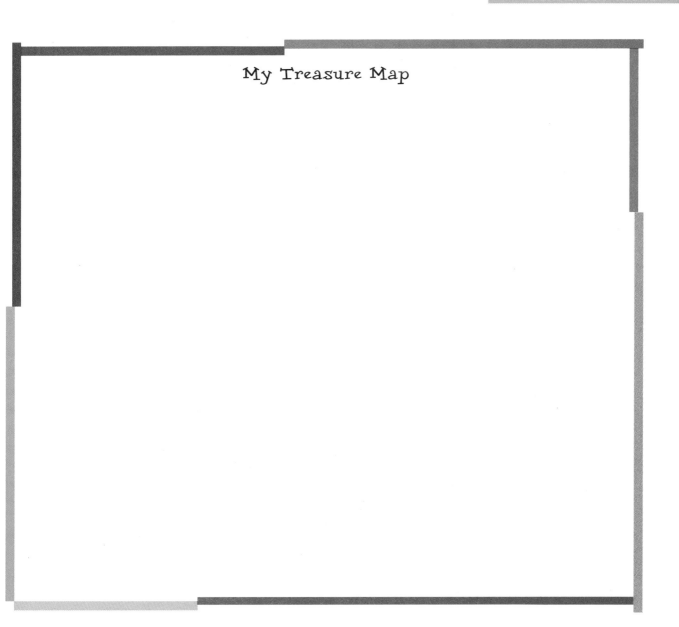

Hunt for Treasure

Have your leader hide a prize in the area right around your camp. Find a partner. Draw a map of the camp and the area around it. Your leader will put an "X" on your map where she hid the treasure. Wait for the rest of the teams to finish their maps. Then, at the same time, every team will start to look for the treasure. May the best map-reading team win!

Who Lives There?

During a hike, look for animal homes. How do you think that the animal built its home? You might see a spider web or a bird nest or the entrance to an underground home.

Leave It Better

Think about what you do outdoors before you act. What does your action do to the environment? Try not to harm the environment.

Wherever you are, city or country, always try to leave a place just the way you found it. Or help to leave a place better than the way you found it.

ACTivity! Read the story that follows about Troop 504. Are the Girl Scouts in the story harming or helping the environment? Circle all of the places in the story where you feel Jennifer, Naomi, Maria, and Kristen may be harming the environment.

Discuss with your leader and troop what the girls could be doing instead. Remember, they should be leaving the place the way they found it or better.

Jennifer, Naomi, Maria, and Kristen were very excited. They were going to the Girl Scout camp for the first time to sleep overnight. They couldn't wait to set up tents and curl up in sleeping bags and have a cookout!

The troop arrived early on Saturday morning. After the girls helped to set up camp, their leaders, Mrs. Gonzalez and Ms. Smith, asked the girls if they would like to go on a nature hike. They all agreed and off they went!

Jennifer and Naomi ran ahead and went off the trail. As Maria walked along, she kicked at loose pieces of dirt and grass.

Kristen was busy eating candy and dropping the wrappers on the ground.

Up ahead, Jennifer and Naomi yelled in excitement.

They had stepped in a patch of beautiful wildflowers. All four girls picked the flowers to take back to camp. Kristen even put a few in her hair.

Later that day, Mrs. Gonzalez and the girls got ready to cook their dinner. They wanted to make a really big fire. The girls collected every piece of old wood lying on the ground around the camp.

They even broke branches off the smaller bushes and trees.

During dinner, Maria dropped her food on the ground in camp. She didn't clean up the mess. Naomi didn't like her dinner so she threw it under a nearby bush.

It was a windy night. All of the paper napkins blew off the table. No one picked them up. So they blew away into the forest.

After dinner, the girls washed the dishes with plenty of soap. They carried the dishwater down to the stream. Jennifer dumped it into the water and walked away.

Everyone was tired. The whole troop went to sleep after singing some Girl Scout songs. Ms. Smith put some more big pieces of wood onto the really big campfire before going to sleep in her tent.

The next day they had to leave the campsite after breakfast. The girls took down their tents. They were very happy with their first campout. Troop 504 couldn't wait to do it again.

What things did the girls do wrong while they were on their nature hike? What about when they were in the camp?

- Jennifer and Naomi should not have run off the hiking trail. Maria shouldn't have kicked the soil and the grass as she walked. They were all crushing the plants and causing the trail to get wider. If the plants die, the soil will wash away.

- Kristen should not have been throwing her candy wrappers on the ground. If she put them in her pocket or day pack, she could have thrown them away in a trash can at camp.
- If you pick wildflowers, you are taking them away from the wildlife that may depend on them for food. The wildflowers also may be endangered species. Besides, there will be none left for other people to enjoy.
- There is no need to make a big campfire. In fact, using a portable stove to cook would be better for the environment.

Old tree branches and other pieces of wood and bark are important to the habitat. They put nutrients back into the soil. They provide hiding places for small creatures. Breaking twigs and branches from living bushes and trees weakens them. They could die from disease.

- You should never leave a fire unattended. Never go to sleep without first putting out your campfire.
- Maria, Jennifer, and the others did not try to keep their campsite clean. If food is left on the ground, it will attract wildlife.

Troop 504 did not leave this natural place better than they found it! In fact, if lots of people acted this way, there would not be many places left in nature to enjoy, and plants and animals would have a hard time surviving.

By now, you've really gotten out there into your community and your environment! You may have participated in a service project. You have learned how to conserve natural resources like land and water, and to leave an outdoor place better than the way you found it. All of these wonderful first adventures have helped you to discover more about yourself, too.

In the next chapter, you'll get a peek into how people live in other countries.

Books You Might Like to Read

BOOKS

Amsel, Sheri. *A Wetland Walk*. Brookfield, Conn.: The Millbrook Press, 1993.

Brown, Marc. *Arthur's Neighborhood*. New York: Random House, 1996.

Carlson, Laurie. *Kids Camp!* Chicago, Ill.: Chicago Review Press, 1995.

Dr. Seuss. *The Lorax*. New York: Random House, 1971.

Houk, Randy. *Chessie, The Travelin' Man*. Fairfield, Conn.: The Benefactory, 1997.

Kohl, MaryAnn, and Cindy Gainer. *Good Earth Art: Environmental Art for Kids*. Bellingham, Wash.: Bright Ring Publishing, 1991.

Rylant, Cynthia. *The Bookshop Dog*. New York: Scholastic, 1996.

Schecter, Ellen. *The Big Idea*. New York: Hyperion, 1996.

Schwartz, Linda. *My Earth Book: Puzzles, Projects, Facts, and Fun*. Santa Barbara, Calif.: The Learning Works, Inc., 1991.

Shedd, Warner. *The Kids' Wildlife Book*. Charlotte, Vt.: Williamson, 1994.

Spiotta-DiMare, Loren. *Caesar: On Deaf Ears*. Fairfield, Conn.: The Benefactory, 1997.

Van Cleave, Janice. *Animals: Spectacular Science Projects*. New York: John Wiley, 1993.

Chapter
5

P E O P L E NEAR AND FAR

People Near and Far

Bonjour, Hola, Ciao, Shalom, Yahtahey, Namask, Nihao, Hello. These are just some of the ways people around the world greet each other.

Meet Nada, Eeva, and Carmen. They all came to the United States from very different places in the world. They are Americans now, but they have a lot to tell you about the countries where they were born. Read on and learn about these three girls.

Nada

Hello, my name is Nada. I am from Morocco. It is in northwestern Africa. People who live in Morocco are called Moroccans. Kings have ruled Morocco for over a thousand years. Rubies, amber, gold, and other precious stones were set in the walls of their royal palaces, and beautiful tiles covered both the floors and walls.

I once lived in a town called El Jadida, near the Atlantic Ocean. It was built in the 1600s. Walls enclose the entire town.

My house in Morocco was very different from my house here in America. It was built in a circle, and the rooms opened up to an outdoor yard. The yard has a small garden with lemon trees and geraniums and a little water fountain in the center. It was our family room. On warm evenings, my family spent most of the time there.

Moroccan homes often have beautiful artwork known as mosaics. Mosaics are designs made from colorful tiles. Some of the floors and walls in my house in Morocco were covered with mosaics.

Picture Mosaics

ACTivity! You can create your own mosaic.

Materials:
- Poster board or cardboard.
- Scissors.
- Glue in a squeeze bottle.
- Glitter.
- Lots of colorful scrap paper—
  construction paper, Sunday funnies,
  magazine pages, shiny wrapping paper
  (use old wrapping paper), old coloring
  book pages.

Directions:

Cut the colorful paper into small squares.
These are your paper tiles. Sketch a simple
design on the poster board or cardboard.

Glue on the squares to fill up the empty
spaces of your picture. You may leave a
little space between the paper tiles.

Squeeze a little glue between the paper
tiles.

Sprinkle glitter to fill in these spaces
between the paper. The glitter will attach
to the glue on your picture.

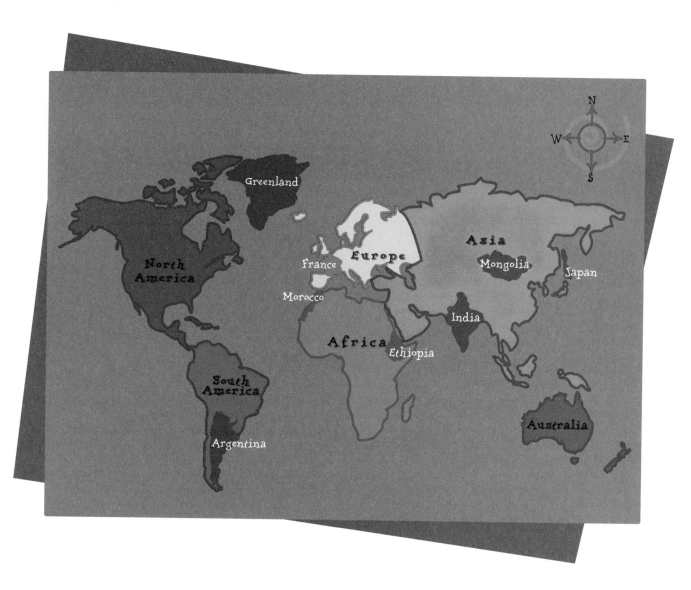

Find Morocco

First find Africa on the map. Then look at the northern part of Africa. Now look a little to the west (look left). Morocco is there.

I can read and write in Arabic, and I know some French. Since I have been in the United States for two years, I have also learned how to speak English.

Like my family, I am a Muslim. I worship Allah, which means God in the Arabic language. My place of worship is called a *mosque*. My favorite food is couscous. Couscous is the national dish of Morocco. It is a wheat grain food that Moroccans steam. I like to eat it with vegetables like squash, tomatoes, and carrots. Some people also eat it with lamb.

I also like dates. They are very sweet fruit that grow in the hot deserts of southern Morocco. Have you ever tasted a date? You can buy some dates in a supermarket and try this recipe:

Nada's Favorite Rice Pudding with Dates

- 2 cups cooked white rice.
- 15 pitted dates, chopped finely.
- 2 cups low-fat milk.
- 3 tablespoons sugar.

In a blender, mix the rice until thick. Place the rice in a large pan. Add the other ingredients. Cover the pan and cook on low heat for 15–20 minutes.

Moroccans often eat their food with their hands. When we do this, we have to obey very strict rules.

ACTivity! You have learned several new words that relate to my culture. Looking up, down, and following diagonally, find the following words hidden among the letters: Arabic, couscous, Morocco, mosaic, mosque, Muslim, tiles. See page 128 for the answers.

S	E	C	A	F	T	A	N
S	U	E	Q	A	R	T	M
S	Q	O	T	M	U	I	A
E	S	N	C	O	L	L	R
R	O	A	F	S	O	E	A
I	M	F	U	A	U	S	B
U	B	M	L	I	E	O	I
M	O	R	O	C	C	O	C

Eeva

Hello, my name is Eeva. I am from Finland. I think my country is the most beautiful in the world. It is called "land of a thousand lakes." My home was in the village of Utsjoki near the Arctic Circle. It is in an area of Finland called Lapland. Do you know where the Arctic Circle is? Try to find Lapland on a map or globe.

Utsjoki is dark all day as well as all night from November to the middle of January. Those months are called *kaamos*, which means *polar night*. Because there is very

little sun, the weather is very cold. I prefer the summer months. That's when Utsjoki has daylight all day and all night!

A Finnish Village During Kaamos

Draw a picture of a snowy winter village where the sun does not rise. It would look something like the hours before dawn.

People from Finland are called Finnish. My family belongs to the group of Finnish people called *Saame*. I speak the Saame language. My classes were taught in Saame so that the language wouldn't die out. I also speak Finnish.

In Finland, we kept herds of reindeer, and used reindeer fur for clothing. Years ago, reindeer were used for transportation. They pulled sleighs over the snow. Now the Saame use snowmobiles.

My home in Finland was a one-level brick house. Like most of my Finnish friends, my family had a sauna. A sauna is a kind of bath. You sit in a very hot room. The heat is produced by small amounts of water dropped on stones that have been heated. I took a sauna bath after my shower at least twice a week. Here in America, I miss my sauna.

A Lapland Felt Design

ACTivity! When I lived near the Arctic Circle, I wore bright blue clothing made of felt. Red and yellow felt designs were on the clothing. People dressed in bright colors so they could be seen on the white snow. You can make a felt square with designs on it like the ones worn in Lapland.

Materials:
- A square of bright blue felt.
- Scraps of red and yellow felt.
- Sewing scraps: rickrack, braiding, seam binding.
- White glue.
- Pencil, ruler, scissors.

Directions:
1. Draw triangles on the scraps of red and yellow felt. Use your ruler to make the lines straight. Cut out the triangles.
2. Cut out yellow and red bands from the scraps.
3. Place the triangles and the bands on the blue felt square.
4. Make a design that you like.
5. Add the scraps and trim you haven't used.
6. When you like the final design, glue the felt pieces on the square. Let the glue dry overnight.

You can hang your felt square or put it on a table.

Carmen

Hi, my name is Carmen. I am from Peru. My people are called Peruvians and speak Spanish. Find Peru on a map. It is in South America.

I am very proud of the country where I was born. Peruvians might live near an ocean, a rain forest, a coastal desert, or the Andes Mountains. I lived in the town of Cuzco, near the Andes Mountains.

In the United States, I attend a bilingual school. That's a school where both English and Spanish are spoken. My English has improved a lot. I also speak a language called *Quechua*. It is the ancient Inca language.

My ancestors are the Incas. The Incas ruled all the lands around Peru more than four hundred years ago. They built over 10,000 miles of roads and many big cities, some of them high in the mountains. Today, people visit the ruins of these ancient cities.

I have just joined a Brownie Girl Scout troop in the United States. In Peru, I was an Alita. That is what Brownie Girl Scouts are called. Alita means *Little Wing*.

This how the Girl Scout Promise is written in Spanish:

La Promesa de las Girl Scouts

Por mi honor, yo trataré:

De servir a Dios y a mi patria,

Ayudar a las personas en todo momento,

Y vivir conforme a la Ley de las

Girl Scouts.

I taught my Brownie Girl Scout troop how to say the Promise in Spanish.

In Peru, the flute has always been a very popular instrument. Ancient jars and vases are decorated with drawings of flutes. From these we know that flutes were used many years ago in hunting, dancing, and ceremonies. The Incas made flutes of gold and silver. They were called *kenas*. Now the flutes are made of wood.

Los Maizales

Folk Song

Los mai - za - les bro - tan con pri - mor
ful - gu - ran sus ho - jas de co - lor; La tie - rra fer - til,
el sol be - só, su be - llo gra - no ger - mi - nó.
Tie - rra Pe - rua - na de ho - nor te em - bria - gas.

2. Después de la faena intelectual
vamos presurosos a jugar,
Cual nuestros padres al son de pan,
vamos el campo a cultivar.
Tierra Peruana, de honor te embriagas

This song describes the beauty of the corn-fields and suggests that all Peruvians should help with the task of "growing their bread."

Role Play ACTivity!

Pretend that Nada, Eeva, or Carmen has just joined your Girl Scout troop. Play a scene where two girls are speaking to her and trying to get to know her. Introduce her to your troop and try to make her welcome.

Hands Across America

Your country, the United States of America, is a place where people come from all over the world. It is a country of American Indians, Moroccans like Nada, Finns like Eeva, Peruvians like Carmen, and many others.

Your family may have recently come to America from another country, or may have come many years ago. But whenever they came, your family became Americans. Nada, Eeva, and Carmen have all become Americans.

Americans from these different cultures, races, and religions meet each other at school, at work, at the neighborhood store, at restaurants, movie theaters, the mall, and many other places.

I Have an Ancestor Who...

An ancestor is a relative who lived many years ago. She is no longer alive, but you can learn something about her from older relatives who are still living. They may have photographs of her or letters written by her, or other items that will give you some idea of what she was like. They may also have strong memories of her to share with you.

Learn something about one of your ancestors. Come to your next troop or group meeting prepared to tell something about her. You can start your story with "I have an ancestor who…" or any way you wish.

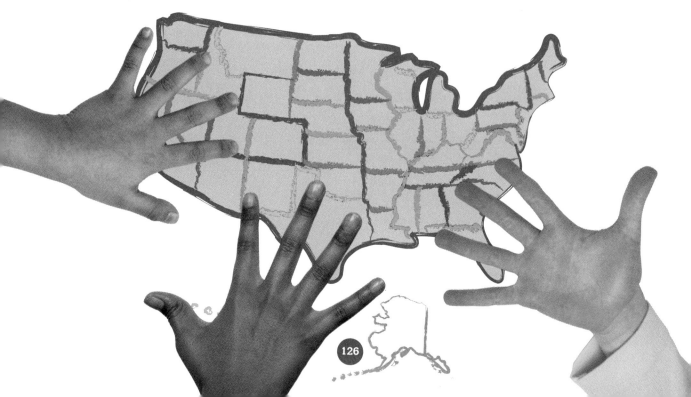

Our Global Community

Plan a special service project to help people in your community, in another part of this country, or in other countries. Ask your leader to help you find a place where people need clothing, food, first-aid kits, or school supplies.

The chart on this page will help organize your thoughts. Check page 92 for more ideas about doing service projects.

Name of Project _____

1. Name the problem.

_____
_____
_____
_____

2. Make a list of actions and solutions.

_____
_____
_____
_____

3. Pick one that will work best.

_____
_____
_____

4. Decide how to do the project.

• Think carefully about the project.
• What will be done?
• Will it cost money?
• When will it be done?
• Is it too hard to do? Can we divide the project into smaller parts?
• Who will help us? Can we get other people in the community to help?
• How much time will we need?

_____
_____
_____

5. Do it!

6. Think about what we accomplished.

7. Share what we did with others.

Fighting Prejudice

Some people are afraid of or dislike others who are different from them. Isn't it silly not to like someone you don't even know? This bad feeling is called *prejudice*. People are not born with prejudice. But often people learn to be prejudiced as they grow up.

When you say the Girl Scout Law, you promise to be a sister to every Girl Scout. She may be taller than you. She may have a different skin color. Her family might practice a different religion. When you say the Girl Scout Law, you agree to try to get along with all of these girls.

Sometimes, no matter how you try to get along with others, it doesn't work. You might say something in anger, or hurt somebody's feelings by mistake. Or somebody might say something that hurts you.

Dr. M tries to help girls who write to her on the Girl Scout Web site (www.girlscouts.org/girls). She has gotten letters like this one about acts of prejudice:

ACTivity! You can write your own letter to Dr. M. See the section on cyberspace on page__. But remember, she gets so many letters that she can only answer a couple of them on the Web site each week.

Dear Dr. M,

Yesterday in the school lunchroom, Erica called the new Chinese girl in our class a bad name. I told her that she shouldn't talk that way about people. Erica got mad. My other friends sided with her against me. Now none of them will talk to me. They're all saying things about me.

Signed,

No Friends

Dear No Friends,

You stood up for what you believe. That is a very good thing. But it's not always easy. You were right. Too many people remain silent when others say bad things about other people. Name-calling will continue until people like you speak out against it. In time, your friends, maybe even Erica, will come around. And you might make a new friend or two who will be proud to know someone as courageous as you.

Dr. M

We're the Same/ We're Different

How can two girls be similar and different at the same time? They may be similar because they're girls. But their skin color might be different.

With a partner, sit or stand facing each other. Think of three ways the two of you are alike. Then think of three ways you are different. Be sure to discover things other than how you look. Share your similarities and your differences with your entire group.

Games from Around the World

Children from all over the world love to play games. Here are some favorite Brownie Girl Scout games from other countries.

Rabbit Without a House (Brazil)

This game from Brazil is best when you have at least 11 people.

1. Pick someone to be "it" (the rabbit without a house) and someone to be the caller.
2. Divide the others into groups of three.
3. Each group makes a rabbit in a house by two girls holding hands (the house) and one girl (the rabbit) standing inside.
4. The caller yells out "Find a house" and all the rabbits, including the one without a house, have to run to find another house.
5. The rabbit left without a house becomes it.

Mr. Bear (Sweden)

You'll need at least three people, a place for "home," and the bear's den.

1. One person is Mr. Bear. He is trying to sleep in his den.
2. The other players sneak up to Mr. Bear and whisper, "Mr. Bear, are you awake?"
3. Mr. Bear pretends not to hear them. Then the players yell, "MR. BEAR, ARE YOU AWAKE?" This makes Mr. Bear furious! He chases them all and tries to catch them before they reach home, which is the safe place.
4. Everyone tagged by the bear before reaching home becomes one of Mr. Bear's cubs. They go back to the den with Mr. Bear.
5. When the remaining players come back to wake up Mr. Bear again, the cubs help Mr. Bear catch them.
6. When everyone has been caught, someone else becomes Mr. Bear.

The United States of America

Now you know a lot more about different kinds of people. Your country, the United States of America, is made up of people from all parts of the world. The United States is like a mosaic made up of many different little pieces that come together to make a beautiful picture.

United States of America Collage

You can use many different things to make your own collage of the United States of America.

Materials:
- Pictures of mountains, forests, lakes, cities, deserts, beaches, and other scenes.
- Your own drawings and words that describe how we all live in this country.
- Poster board.
- Scissors.
- Glue.

Directions:
Place the pictures you have cut out and your own drawings on the poster. Try different positions for the items until you find the one you like best. Then glue everything in place.

Many Hands Across America Paper Dolls

ACTivity! Make paper dolls that are as different from each other as the many people who live in the United States.

Directions:
1. Take a sheet of paper that is about the same size as the pages in this book.
2. Fold the end over two inches like an accordion, back and forth until the entire paper is folded.

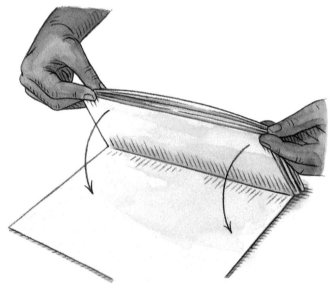

3. Hold the folded paper together and draw half a person on the top fold. Make sure the arms and legs touch the fold.

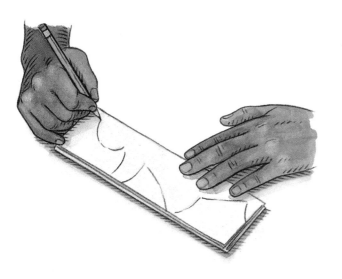

5. Open it up. The paper dolls should be attached and holding hands. Color each doll with different skin, hair, and clothing. For fun, glue on actual faces cut from magazines. (Find faces from different races.) You can use a photo of your own face, too. Bits of fabric or colorful paper from magazines can be added for the clothing and hair.

4. Cut the lines of your drawing carefully. Cut through all folded sections.

You can display your dolls across a map of the United States.

Paalam, Au Revoir,

Mi Gaan, Kwa Heri,

Adiós, Good-Bye!

Books You Might Like to Read

Altman, Linda Jacobs. *Amelia's Road.* New York: Lee and Low, 1995. Available in Spanish.

Atkins, Jeannine. *Aani and the Tree Huggers.* New York: Lee and Low, 1995.

Barber, Barbara E. *Allie's Basketball Dream.* New York: Lee and Low, 1996.

Beatty, Theresa M. *Food and Recipes of the Caribbean.* New York: Rosen/Powerkids Press, 1998.

Cha, Dia. *Dia's Story Cloth.* New York: Lee and Low, 1998.

Fine, Edith Hope. *Under the Lemon Moon.* New York: Lee and Low, 1999.

Hamilton, Virginia. *Her Stories.* New York: Blue Sky Press, 1996.

Haugen, Tormod. *Keeping Secrets* (translated from Norwegian). New York: HarperCollins, 1994.

Kavasch, E. Barrie, ed. *Zuni Children and Their Elders Talk Together.* New York: Rosen/Powerkids Press, 1998.

Marston, Elsa. *The Cliffs of Cairo.* Cairo, Egypt: Hoopoe Books, 1998. Distributed by AMIDEAST.

Martin, Jacqueline Briggs. *Snowflake Bently.* New York: Houghton Mifflin, 1998.

Meers, Trevor. *101 Best Web Sites for Kids.* Lincolnwood, Ill.: Publications International, 1999.

Miller, William. *A House by the River.* New York: Lee and Low, 1997.

Nikola-Lisa. *Bein' with You This Way.* New York: Lee and Low, 1994. Also available in Spanish.

Ringgold, Faith. *Aunt Harriet's Underground Railroad in the Sky.* New York: Crown, 1993.

San Soucci, Daniel. *Cindrillon: A Caribbean Cinderella.* New York: Simon and Schuster, 1998.

Sis, Peter. *Tibet: Through the Red Box.* New York: Farrar Straus Giroux, 1998.

Stalcup, Ann. *Japanese Origami: Paper Magic.* New York: Rosen/Powerkids Press, 1999.

Trumbauer, Lisa. *Computer Fun.* Brookfield, Conn.: The Millbrook Press, 1999.

Williams, Sherley Anne. *Working Cotton.* New York: Voyager Picture Books, 1997.

Becoming a Junior Girl Scout

How is being a Junior Girl Scout different from being a Brownie Girl Scout? Here's the chance to find out. Sample some Junior Girl Scout activities, find out about the Junior Girl Scout uniform and Junior badges, and do some fun activities with Junior Girl Scouts.

When Girl Scouts move from one age level to another, it's called *bridging*. As a Brownie Girl Scout, you may have remembered bridging from Daisy Girl Scouts. Your Brownie Girl Scout wings show you have completed your years at this age level. You are ready to *fly up* to Junior Girl Scouting. This is a tradition that goes back to when Brownie Girl Scout leaders were called *Brown Owls*.

Earning Your Bridge to Junior Girl Scouts Award

Every Brownie Girl Scout receives her wings at the end of her Brownie Girl Scout years. Some girls also choose to earn their Bridge to Junior Girl Scouts rainbow. You will need to pick at least **one** activity from each of the six steps to Junior Girl Scouting to learn what is at the end of your bridging rainbow. Get started and see!

1. Find Out About Junior Girl Scouting.
- Ask a Junior Girl Scout or an adult who works with Junior Girl Scouts to tell you about Junior Girl Scouting.
- Find out about the awards (badges and signs) for Junior Girl Scouts by looking at a Junior Girl Scout sash, vest, catalog picture, or the Just for Girls Web pages at www.girlscouts.org/girls. Look through the *Junior Girl Scout Handbook* and *Girl Scout Badges and Signs*. Find out about the badges, the signs, and the leadership pin. Look for differences between Brownie and Junior Girl Scout activities.
- Take part in a special event put on by your community service unit, council, or a Junior Girl Scout troop for Brownie Girl Scouts bridging to the Junior level.

2. Do a Junior Girl Scout Activity.
- Do an activity from the *Junior Girl Scout Handbook* or *Girl Scout Badges and Signs*.
- Do an activity from a Junior Girl Scout Issues for Girl Scouts booklet, such as *Connections, Read to Lead, Girls Are Great,* or *Media Know-How.*
- Do a Junior Girl Scout online science or technology activity on the Just for Girls Web pages (www.girlscouts.org).

3. Do something with a Junior Girl Scout or a Junior Girl Scout troop or group.
- Attend a meeting or event as the guest of a Junior Girl Scout troop or group.
- Do a service project with Junior Girl Scouts.
- Write to a Junior Girl Scout pen pal (mail) or key pal (e-mail) who lives in your area or another state.

4. **Share what you learn about Junior Girl Scouting with Brownie or Daisy Girl Scouts.**

- Make a poster or collage, or create a poster or flier on the computer, to show others what Junior Girl Scouts is all about.
- Put on a skit or special program about a service project or activity that you did with a Junior Girl Scout.
- Teach a song or game that you learned from a Junior Girl Scout.

5. **Plan and do a summer Girl Scout activity.**

(If your Brownie Girl Scout troop or group has its bridging ceremony before summer, you can receive your Bridge to Junior Girl Scouts award before doing this activity. However, you should do the activity before your first Junior Girl Scout meeting in the fall.)

- Go to Girl Scout day or resident (sleep away) camp.
- Plan and do an outdoor activity with other Girl Scouts and their families.
- Have a cookout, swim or skate party, campfire, or stargazing activity with other Girl Scouts.
- Participate in a *GirlSports* activity with other Girl Scouts.
- Plan a get-acquainted activity for fall for your new Junior Girl Scout troop buddies.

- Write a summer newsletter.
- Do a service project with other Girl Scouts.

6. **Help plan your fly-up ceremony.**

- Learn a new opening or closing that you can use in your flying-up ceremony.
- Write a poem, song, or skit about going from Brownie to Junior Girl Scouts that you can use in your ceremony.
- Design and make invitations for the ceremony.
- Make decorations that you can use at the ceremony.

Your Brownie Girl Scout Memories

You might want to take some time to fill in your Brownie Girl Scout memories before you move on to Junior Girl Scouts. Look back from the other side of the bridging rainbow. Remember all of the fun things that you have accomplished as a Brownie Girl Scout.

Encourage your friends to join you as you become a Junior Girl Scout, or wait for them on the other side if they are younger. Say good-bye to being a Brownie, and hello to the world of Junior Girl Scouting!

ACTivity!

My Brownie Girl Scout Memories

I have been a Brownie Girl Scout during these years: ....

....

My favorite Try-Its were ....

....

....

....

....

My favorite field trips were ....

....

....

....

My favorite service projects were ....
....
....
....

I felt like a leader when I ....
....
....
....

I am proudest of ....
....
....
....

My leaders were ....
....
....
....

I had fun when we ....
....
....
....

The words I would use to describe my Brownie Girl Scout troop are ....
....
....
....

The girls who were in my troop were ....
....
....
....

139

Index